Tolkien and Philosophy

Tolkien and Philosophy

edited by
Roberto Arduini & Claudio A. Testi

2014

Cormarë Series No. 32

Series Editors: Peter Buchs • Thomas Honegger • Andrew Moglestue • Johanna Schön

Series Editor responsible for this volume: Thomas Honegger

Library of Congress Cataloging-in-Publication Data

Roberto Arduini and Claudio A. Testi (eds.):
Tolkien and Philosophy
ISBN 978-3-905703-32-0

Italian edition: Tolkien e la Filosofia. Genoa and Milan: Marietti *1820*. First edition 2011.

Subject headings:
Tolkien, J.R.R. (John Ronald Reuel), 1892-1973
Philosophy
Death and Immortality
Inklings
The Lord of the Rings
The Hobbit
The Silmarillion

Cormarë Series No. 32

First published 2014

© Walking Tree Publishers, Zurich and Jena, 2014
The text of Wu Ming 4 in "Tolkien the Catholic Philosopher?" © 2013 by Wu Ming 4
Published by arrangement with Roberto Santachiara Literary Agency

All rights reserved. No portion of this book may be reproduced, by any process or technique, without the express written consent of the publisher

Cover illustration 'The Phial of Galadriel' by Anke Eissmann.
Reproduced by permission of the artist. Copyright 2001.

Set in Adobe Garamond Pro and Shannon by Walking Tree Publishers
Printed by Lightning Source in the United Kingdom and United States

Board of Advisors

Academic Advisors

Douglas A. Anderson (independent scholar)

Dieter Bachmann (Universität Zürich)

Patrick Curry (independent scholar)

Michael D.C. Drout (Wheaton College)

Vincent Ferré (Université de Paris-Est Créteil UPEC)

Verlyn Flieger (University of Maryland)

Thomas Fornet-Ponse (Rheinische Friedrich-Wilhelms-Universität Bonn)

Christopher Garbowski (University of Lublin, Poland)

Mark T. Hooker (Indiana University)

Andrew James Johnston (Freie Universität Berlin)

Rainer Nagel (Johannes Gutenberg-Universität Mainz)

Helmut W. Pesch (independent scholar)

Tom A. Shippey (University of Winchester)

Allan G. Turner (Friedrich-Schiller-Universität Jena)

Frank Weinreich (independent scholar)

General Readers

Johan Boots

Jean Chausse

Friedhelm Schneidewind

Isaac Juan Tomas

Patrick Van den hole

Johan Vanhecke (Letterenhuis, Antwerp)

Acknowledgments

Many thanks to all those who worked with us to make this volume possible, and especially Alberto Ladavas who helped us with the revision of the proofs.

A great 'thank you' also to the WTP interns who helped layouting and proofreading the text and who proved expert typo-hunters: Stephanie Luther, Olga Pisanaia, Luise Wendler, and Stefanie Schneider.

Thomas Honegger, Roberto Arduini & Claudio Testi

Contents

Roberto Arduini & Claudio A. Testi
Introduction — 9

Franco Manni & Tom Shippey
Tolkien between Philosophy and Philology — 21

Verlyn Flieger
Tolkien and the Philosophy of Language — 73

Andrea Monda & Wu Ming 4
Tolkien the Catholic Philosopher? — 85

Christopher Garbowski
Tolkien's Philosophy and Theology of Death — 125

Giampaolo Canzonieri
Tolkien at King Edward's School — 145

Index — 153

Roberto Arduini[1] & Claudio A. Testi[2]

Introduction

Tethered in a basket floating in the air above "The Thoughtery", withdrawn and severed from the real world in his own abstract universe, that's how Socrates, most renowned among philosophers, is portrayed by Aristophanes in "The Clouds", a comedy of his dating back to 423 BC.

Two and a half millennia later that is still the way philosophers and philosophy look to the common imagination as, in a way, does Professor Tolkien, whom many still imagine as a white-haired, patronizing old gentleman superciliously looking at the real world from an Oxford high-table in the few moments when he is not lost in imaginary worlds of his own or, even more abstruse, in inventing imaginary languages.

Of course *we* know none of this is true, that this trite, stereotyped image applies neither to Tolkien not to the masters of the "Art of thinking", and yet what they really have in common has seldom, if ever, been analyzed in Tolkien-centred secondary literature.

"Tolkien and Philosophy", we deem, is a theme that has not yet been studied with the "philological" accuracy and the textual knowledge that are required to avoid hammering the Professor's works inside conceptual frameworks that, rather than exposing their intrinsic value, could instead put them at risk of losing, in the eyes of the readers, both their profound meaning and their inherent beauty.

In what relation does Tolkien's work stand with respect to Philosophy? The question, if taken seriously, is by no means trivial. If it is well known that Tolkien is essentially a philologist, in fact, it is also true that inside his works, both literary and philological, there are plenty of truly authentic philosophical

---

1 Associazione Romana di Studi Tolkieniani
2 Istituto Filosofico di Studi Tomistici

themes to be found, such as Power, Evil, Death and Deathlessness, Paganism, Christianity, and the relationship of the latter to the former themes, Time and Memory, Technology and Nature, the origin of Myth and Language, and many more. However, how many specific studies have been dedicated to the subtle relationships between Tolkien and philosophical thinking? To get an idea we searched the most comprehensive bibliographical resources[3] for titles including either words such as "philosophy", "theology", "psychology" and their derivatives ("philosophical", etc.), or names of authors pertaining to those subjects. Results proved that only 1,33% of the searched titles satisfied the adopted criteria (62 out of about 4.679), a very small percentage which, when put in relation to the (almost) six decades covered (58 years from 1954 to 2012), means that hardly more than one title per year (1,1) published. In addition, 24 out of 62 titles have been published after 2001, i.e. after the first of Peter Jackson's movies and the resulting new interest in Tolkien. Of course the reported data could, and should, be further refined, yet they clearly show that criticism has more or less ignored the subject of Tolkien and Philosophy, philosophers, and other related disciplines.

Turning again to the 62 titles, of course we cannot claim to have read all of them, the older ones being exceedingly difficult to access. Nevertheless, having read 85% of the works listed after 2001, we feel we can say that none had the direct and explicit goal of studying the relationships between Tolkien and Western thought and that, in the end, the critical works specifically centred on uncovering the relationships between Tolkien and philosophical thinking by thoroughly analysing sources and texts are admittedly almost inexistent. Moreover, as far as meetings and conventions are concerned, we feel we can say that the first to be entirely dedicated to the theme of Tolkien and Philosophy has indeed been the one whose proceedings you are about to read, held in Modena in May 2010 thanks the joined effort of *Istituto Filosofico di Studi Tomistici* and *Associazione Romana di Studi Tolkieniani*.

---

3 Namely, the Tolkien Studies, *Tolkien criticism: an annotated checklist* by Richard C. West (1970), *J.R.R. Tolkien: six decades of criticism* by Judith Anne Johnson (1986), "Tom Shippey's *J.R.R. Tolkien: Author of the Century* and a look back at Tolkien criticism since 1982" by Michael D.C. Drout, in *Envoi* 9.2 (2000), "Scholarly Studies of J.R.R. Tolkien and His Work (in English): 1984-2000" by Michael D.C. Drout, in *Envoi* 9.2 (Fall 2000) and, for the Italian scholarship, *Bibliografia dei libri su Tolkien* by Lorenzo Gammarelli, available at http://www.soronel.it/.

In agreement with the Editors – *Marietti* 1820 and *Walking Tree Publishers*, for the Italian and the English version, respectively – we decided to keep the lecturers' contributions in the original "conversational" form, both in the case of the two debates between Franco Manni and Tom Shippey and Andrea Monda and Wu Ming 4, and the separate lectures given by Verlyn Flieger and Christopher Garbowsky. We deem this form not only to better reflect the authentic "dialogic" nature of the meeting, but also better suited to let the readers appreciate the quality of the contributions that sometimes mark, in our opinion, a "fundamental" point in research on the complex theme of Tolkien and Philosophy. For those reasons, rather than summarizing each contribution, we prefer to diachronically list the various themes that can be found inside the proceedings:

- young Tolkien's philosophical education at secondary school (145-150) and university (27, 27 nn.10-11);
- the term "Philosophy" as used by Tolkien (21-22);
- philosophers' names quoted by Tolkien (21-22, 24);
- philosophical influences in Tolkien's works (27-33, 34-35, 44-45, 51-52);
- differences in methodology between Philosophy and Philology (22-26; 34-35);
- importance of Philosophy for some philologists (34-42);
- philosophy of Myth and Language according to Tolkien (73-83);
- Tolkien as thinker and narrator (85-87, 93-94);
- the meaning and possibility of a Christian literature (90-93);
- Tolkien as a Christian/Catholic (94-97, 99-100, 128) or a non-Catholic (96) narrator;
- Tolkien and Theology (88, 125-126, 133);
- Miscellaneous themes: Providence (55-65), Heroism (91, 117-120, 129), modernity of Tolkien's world (115); Power (120), Death (120-122, 125 ff), Tolkien and C.S. Lewis (41, 49-50, 51), the Inklings and the Bloomsbury Group (52-54), Paganism and Christianity (101-102, 115), narration and action (105-109).

In conclusion, let us say that we wish this book to become, in both method and content, an essential point of reference for anyone interested in better understanding the significant connections that sometimes link, sometimes divide, "philologist" Tolkien and the proper philosophical speculation.

Bibliographical Research Concerning Tolkien and Philosophy

Works consulted

DROUT, Michael D.C. and Patrick H. WYNNE. 2000. "Tom Shippey's *J.R.R. Tolkien: Author of the Century* and a Look Back at Tolkien Criticism since 1982." *Envoi* 9.2:101-167.

GAMMARELLI, Lorenzo. *Soronel: Bibliography of Books in Italian on Tolkien*: http://www.soronel.it/S00001.html

JOHNSON, Judith A. 1986. *J.R.R. Tolkien: Six Decades of Criticism*. Bibliographies and Indexes in World Literature 6. Westport, CT: Greenwood Press.

Tolkien Studies, volumes I-X, Section "Bibliography" (2001-2011)

WEST, Richard. 1981. *Tolkien Criticism. An Annotated Checklist (Revised Edition)*. Kent, OH: Kent State University Press.

Criteria

- titles including either words such as "philosophy", "theology", "psychology" and their derivatives ("philosophical", etc.),
- titles including names of authors pertaining to those subjects
- we have not listed individually the essays or chapters in either of the four volumes comprising contributions focussing on philosophy in Tolkien's works (i.e. *The Lord of the Rings and Philosophy*, *The Hobbit and Philosophy*, *La Filosofia del Signore degli Anelli*, and *Tolkien e la Filosofia*) but listed each book once only

62 titles meeting the above criteria

year	author	title	reference
1956	H.M.Y.	"Escathology"	*The Student Movement* (London) 58, 37-38
1956	L.C.S.	"Theosophical News and Notes"	*The Theosophical Journal* March-April, 24
1959	Huppe, Bernard F.	"Conjectures"	Chapter VI in *Doctrine and Poetry: Augustine's Influences on Old English Poetry*. New York: State University of New York
1960	Wright, Marjorie Evelyn	*The Cosmic Kingdom of Myth: A Study in the Myth-Philosophy of Charles Williams, C.S. Lewis, and J.R.R. Tolkien*	Ph.D. dissertation, University of Illinois
1966	Tunick, Barry	"Social Philosophy in *The Lord of the Rings*"	*Tolkien Journal* 2.2, 9
1967	Sklar, Robert	"Tolkien and Hesse: Top of the Pops"	*Nation* 204 (8 May 1967), 598-601
1967	Winter, Karen Corlett	"Grendel, Gollum, and the Un-Man: The Death of the Monster as an Archetype"	*Orcrist* 2 (1967-68), 28-37
1968	Wojcik, Jan S.J.	"Tolkien and Coleridge: Remaking of the 'Green Earth'"	*Renascence*, 20.3 (Spring 1968), 132-39, 146
1969	Duriez, Colin	"Leonardo, Tolkien, and Mr. Baggins"	*Mythlore* 2 (April 1969), 18-28
1969	Kilby, Clyde	"Tolkien and Coleridge"	*Orcrist* 3 [also *Tolkien Journal* 4.1&2] (Spring-Summer 1969), 16-19

year	author	title	reference
1969	O'Hale, Colmán	*The Universe of Order: Some Aspects of the Natural Law in J.R.R.Tolkien's The Lord of the Rings*	M.A. Thesis, University of Waterloo, Ontario, 1969; Phil.M. Thesis University of Waterloo, Ontario, 1970
1969	Urang, Gunnar	"Tolkien's Fantasy: The Phenomenology of Hope"	In Mark R. Hillegas (ed.), 1969. *Shadows of Imagination: The Fantasies of C.S.Lewis, J.R.R.Tolkien and Charles Williams*. Carbondale, IL: Southern Illinois University Press. New ed. 1979, 97-110
1970	Helms, Randell	"The Structure and Aesthetic of Tolkien's *Lord of the Rings*"	*Mythcon I Proceedings* (4-7 September 1970). Ed. Glen GoodKnight. Los Angeles: Mythopoeic Society, 5-8
1970	Helms, Randell	"Orc: The Id in Blake and Tolkien"	*Literature and Psychology* 20.1, 31-35
1973	Muirhead, Rev Jan A.	"Theology in Gandalf's Garden"	*Modern Churchman* 26.2, 118-27
1974	Purtill, Richard	*Lord of the Elves and Eldils: Fantasy and Philosophy in C.S. Lewis and J.R.R. Tolkien*	Grand Rapids, MI: Zondervan Publishing House. 2nd edition: San Francisco: Ignatius Press, 2006
1976	Spice, Wilma Helen	*A Jungian View of Tolkien's 'Gandalf': An Investigation of Enabling and Exploitative Power in Counseling and Psychotherapy from the Viewpoint of Analytical Psychology*	Ph.D. dissertation; University of Pittsburgh
1978	Sardello, Robert J.	"An Empirical-Phenomenological Study on Fantasy with a Note on J.R.R. Tolkien and C.S. Lewis"	*Psychocultural Review* 2, 203-20

year	author	title	reference
1979	Kocher, Paul H.	"Jung in Middle-earth"	*Mythlore*, 6.4 (Fall 1979), 25
1979	O'Neil, Timothy	*The Individuated Hobbit: Jung, Tolkien and the Archetypes of Middle-earth*	Boston: Hougton Mifflin
1979	Zipes, Jack	"The Utopian Function of Fairy Tales and Fantasy: Ernst Bloch the Marxist and J.R.R. Tolkien the Catholic"	Ch.5 in *Breaking of Magic Spell: Radical Theories of Folk and Fairy Tales*. London: Heinemann; Austin, TX: University of Texas Press, 129-59
1980	Morse, Robert E.	"Rings of Power in Plato and Tolkien"	*Mythlore* 7.3, 38
1981	Dubs, Kathleen E.	"Providence, Fate & Chance: Boethian Philosophy in *The Lord of the Rings*"	*Twentieth Century Literature* 27, 34-42. Reprinted in Jane Chance (ed.), 2004. *Tolkien and the Invention of Myth*. Lexington, KT: The University Press of Kentucky, 133-42
1982	Rose, M.C.	"The Christian Platonism of C.S. Lewis, J.R.R. Tolkien and Charles Williams"	In D.J. O'Meara (ed.), 1982. *Neoplatonism and Christian Thought*. Albany: State University of New York Press, 203-12
1983	Cox, John	"Tolkien's Platonic Fantasy"	*Seven* 5, 53-69
1984	Davis, Larry Elton	*A Christian Philosophical Examination of the Picture of Evil in the Writings of J.R.R. Tolkien*	Dissertation, South Western Baptist Theological Seminary, See DAI, 44, 1984, 3712a

year	author	title	reference
1986	Flieger, Verlyn	"Naming the Unnameable: The Neoplatonic 'One' in Tolkien's *Silmarillion*"	In Thomas Halton and Joseph P. Williman (eds.), 1986. *Diakonia: Studies in Honor of Robert T. Meyer.* Washington, DC: Catholic University of America Press, 127-32
1988	Greenman, David	"*The Silmarillion* as Aristotelian Epic-Tragedy"	*Mythlore* 53, 14.3, 20-25
1992	Kotowski, Nathalie and Christian Rendel	"Frodo, Sam and Aragorn in Light of C.G. Jung"	*Inklings: Jahrbuch für Literatur und Asthetik* 10, 145-59
1993	Duriez, Colin	"Sub-creation and Tolkien's Theology of Story"	In K.J. Battarbee (ed.), 1993. *Scholarship and Fantasy.* Turku: University of Turku, 133-50
1994	de Armas, Frederick A.	"Gyges' Ring: Invisibility in Plato, Tolkien and Lope de Vega"	*Journal of the Fantastic in the Arts* 3 (1994), 120-38
1995	Houghton, John William	"Augustine and the Ainulindale"	*Mythlore* 21 (1995), 4-8
1995	Noad, Charles E.	"Frodo and His Spectre: Blakean Resonances in Tolkien"	In Patricia Ann Reynolds and Glen GoodKnight (eds.), 1995. *Proceedings of the J.R.R. Tolkien Centenary Conference.* Milton Keynes: The Tolkien Society, 58-62
1995	Agøy, Nils Ivar	"Quid Hinieldus cum Christo? New Perspectives on Tolkien's Theological Dilemma and His Sub-Creation Theory"	In Patricia Ann Reynolds and Glen GoodKnight (eds.), 1995. *Proceedings of the J.R.R. Tolkien Centenary Conference.* Milton Keynes: The Tolkien Society, 31-38

year	author	title	reference
1995	Olszanski, Tadeusz Andrzej	"Evil and the Evil One in Tolkien's Theology"	In Patricia Ann Reynolds and Glen GoodKnight (eds.), 1995. *Proceedings of the J.R.R. Tolkien Centenary Conference*. Milton Keynes: The Tolkien Society, 298-300
1995	Sandner, David	"The Fall From Grace – Decline and Fall in Middle-earth: Metaphors for Nordic and Christian Theology in *The Lord of the Rings* and *The Silmarillion*"	*Mallorn* 32, 15-20
1997	Sterling, Grant C.	"'The Gift of Death': Tolkien's Philosophy of Mortality"	*Mythlore* 82, 21.4 (1997), 16-18, 38
2003	Bassham, Gregory, Bronson, Eric	*The Lord of the Rings and Philosophy: One Book to Rule Them All*	Chicago: Open Court
2003	Evans, Jonathan	"The Anthropology of Arda: Creation, Theology and the Race of Men"	In Jane Chance (ed.), 2003. *Tolkien the Medievalist*. London: Routledge, 195-224
2004	Burns, Marjorie J.	"Norse and Christian Gods: The Integrative Theology of J.R.R. Tolkien"	In Jane Chance (ed.), 2004. *Tolkien and the Invention of Myth: A Reader*. Lexington: University Press of Kentucky, 163-78
2005	Houghton, John Wm. and Neal K. Keesee	"Tolkien, King Alfred, and Boethius: Platonist Views of Evil in *The Lord of the Rings*"	*Tolkien Studies* 2, 131-59

year	author	title	reference
2005	Kreeft, Peter	*The Philosophy of Tolkien: The Worldview Behind The Lord of the Rings*	San Francisco: Ignatius Press
2005	Fornet-Ponse, Thomas	"Tolkiens Theologie des Todes" ["Tolkien's Theology of Death"]	*Hither Shore* 2, 157-86
2006	Fornet-Ponse, Thomas	"Die steigende Präsenz von Philosophie und Theologie" ["The Increasing Presence of Theology and Philosophy"]	*Hither Shore* 3, 37-50, English summary 209-10
2006	Smith, Ross	"Fitting Sense to Sound: Linguistic Aesthetics and Phonosemantics in the Work of J.R.R. Tolkien"	*Tolkien Studies* 3, 1-20
2008	Bonvecchio, Claudio	"La Filosofia del *Signore degli Anelli* (a cura di)"	*Mimesis*, Milano-Udine, 208
2008	Smith, Ross	"Steiner on Tolkien"	*Tolkien Studies* 5, 185-86
2008	Fornet-Ponse, Thomas	"Theology and Fairy-Stories: A Theological Reading of Tolkien's Shorter Works?"	In Margaret Hiley and Frank Weinreich (eds.), 2008. *Tolkien's Shorter Works: Essays of the Jena Conference 2007.* Zurich and Jena: Walking Tree Publishers, 135-65
2008	McKenzie, Tim	"'I Pity Even His Slaves': Tolkien and the Theology of Evil"	In Sarah Wells (ed.), 2008. *The Ring Goes Ever On: Proceedings of the Tolkien 2005 Conference: 50 Years of The Lord of the Rings.* 2 vols. (Coventry: The Tolkien Society). Vol. 2, 91-98

year	author	title	reference
2008	Stevenson, Shandi	"The Shadow beyond the Firelight: Pre-Christian Archetypes and Imagery Meet Christian Theology in Tolkien's Treatment of Evil and Horror"	In Lynn Forest-Hill (ed.), 2008. *The Mirror Crack'd: Fear and Horror in J.R.R. Tolkien's Major Works*. Newcastle upon Tyne: Cambridge Scholars Publishing, 93-117
2008	Wood, Ralph C.	"The Call to Companionship in J.R.R. Tolkien's *The Lord of the Rings*"	In Ralph C. Wood. *Literature and Theology*. Nashville: Abingdon Press, 25-36
2008	Milbank, Alison	"Tolkien, Chesterton, and Thomism"	In Stratford Caldecott and Thomas Honegger (eds.), 2008. *Tolkien's The Lord of the Rings: Sources of Inspiration*. Zurich and Jena: Walking Tree Publishers, 187-98
2008	Oziewicz, Marek	"From Vico to Tolkien: The Affirmation of Myth against the Tyranny of Reason"	In Stratford Caldecott and Thomas Honegger (eds.), 2008. *Tolkien's The Lord of the Rings: Sources of Inspiration*. Zurich and Jena: Walking Tree Publishers, 113-36
2008	Weinreich, Frank	"Metaphysics of Myth: The Platonic Ontology in 'Mythopoeia'"	In Margaret Hiley and Frank Weinreich (eds.), 2008. *Tolkien's Shorter Works: Essays of the Jena Conference 2007*. Zurich and Jena: Walking Tree Publishers, 325-47
2009	Lief, Jason	"Challenging the Objectivist Paradigm: Teaching Biblical Theology with J.R.R. Tolkien, C.S. Lewis, and Guillermo del Toro"	*Teaching Theology and Religion* 12.4 (October 2009), 321-32

year	author	title	reference
2009	McIntosh, Jonathan S.	*The Flame Imperishable: Tolkien, St. Thomas, and the Metaphysiscs of Faerie*	Dissertation for degree in Doctor of Philosophy, UMI dissertation service
2010	Milburn, Michael	"Coleridge's Definition of Imagination and Tolkien's Definition(s) of Faery"	*Tolkien Studies* 7, 55-66
2011	Arduini, Roberto & Claudio Testi	*Tolkien e la Filosofia*	Milano: Marietti 1820
2011	Lobdell, Jared	"Ymagynatyf and J.R.R. Tolkien's Roman Catholicism, Catholic Theology and Religion in *The Lord of the Rings*"	In Paul Kerry and Sandra Miesel (eds.), 2011. *Light Beyond All Shadows: Religious Experience in Tolkien's Work*, Madison, NJ: Fairleigh Dickinson University Press, 79-97
2011	Milburn, Michael	"Art According to Romantic Theology: Charles Williams' Analysis of Dante Reapplied to J.R.R. Tolkien's 'Leaf by Niggle'"	*Mythlore* 29.3-4 (Spring-Summer 2011), 57-75
2011	Birks, Annie	"Augustinian and Boethian Insights into Tolkien's Shaping of Middle-earth: Predestination, Prescience and Free Will"	*Hither Shore* 8, 132-47
2012	Basham, Gregory & Eric Bronson	*The Hobbit and Philosophy*	Hoboken, NJ: Wiley

Franco Manni & Tom Shippey

Tolkien between Philosophy and Philology

1. "Philosophy" and philosophers in Tolkien's works

Franco Manni

In his works Tolkien never refers to a philosopher by name,[1] neither classical figures such as Socrates, Plato, Aristotle, St. Augustine, Thomas Aquinas, Descartes, Kant, Hegel, Schopenhauer or Marx, nor his contemporaries such as Freud, Bergson, Croce, Dewey, Wittgenstein, Husserl, Popper or Ryle. Several ideas of the *philosophia perennis* (a syncretic compound of ancient and medieval traditions) are also frequently employed, but without reference to sources. You wrote to me saying that, although he had read and knew them, Tolkien never named philosophers such as Plato, Boethius and others due to his anti-Classical prejudices and because he wanted to make use of the neglected native English literature but could find no English medieval philosophers prior to Chaucer.[2]

Tolkien *never* uses the word "philosophy" in his fiction, and in other published works only in six instances (three in the lecture "On Fairy Stories" and three in that on *Beowulf*). In his writings not intended for publication, though, the word does appear – rarely in his *Letters* and but twice in the aborted *The Notion Club Papers*: once in reference to the character Rupert Dolbear (who is also interested in psychoanalysis and often falls asleep during discussions) and once in reference to the character Michael Ramer (a philologist and alter-ego of Tolkien), who says that he is *not* a philosopher, but rather an "experimenter".[3]

---

1 Never in those published during his lifetime; among posthumous works, Plato appears once in *The Notion Club Papers* in the context of the myth of Atlantis, which is connected with that of Númenor (*SD* 249).
2 E-mail 21 August 2009.
3 Cf. Manni (2012:5-10).

These occurrences (or rather non-occurrences) of references to philosophers[4] or the word "philosophy" bring to mind Carpenter's reconstruction of a typical Inklings meeting: when they talk of certain thinkers, they do so polemically, disparaging "contemporary thought". I also think that you, Tom, who claim to be totally ignorant of philosophy, harbour towards it a (latent) polemical attitude and consider that philologists have a "concrete mentality" whereas philosophers have an "abstract mentality".[5] Perhaps you and Tolkien have in mind the abstruse and often basically empty philosophy of 19th century German idealism, 20th century German and French existentialism and the diversely abstruse and differently empty "Oxbridge analytical philosophy" that was already strong in English-speaking academic circles before the Second World War and became dominant afterwards?[6]

What do you think, Tom, about the non-occurrence of philosophers' names or the word "philosophy" in Tolkien's works?

Tom Shippey

There are two reasons I can think of why Tolkien uses the word "philosophy" so rarely, and never mentions any individual philosopher. The first reason is easy to state: Tolkien was not a philosopher, he was a philologist. Indeed he declared himself that he was a "*pure* philologist" (*Letters* no. 153), and the emphasis is Tolkien's. Furthermore, though he did not say this, I would add that he was a pure *comparative* philologist.

I need to explain briefly what these words meant for Tolkien. In the first place, for him "philology" had a much broader sense than the older classical one of studying manuscripts, making collations, and establishing authoritative texts. When "comparative philology" was first thought of, in the early 19th century,

---

4 Their absence is wholly deliberate, I think. For example, in the preparatory versions of the lecture "On Fairy Stories" Tolkien cites Carl G. Jung, while in the definitive version he merely uses the word "archetype", omitting the name of the Zurich psychiatrist (cf. Flieger & Anderson 2008:129, 170, 307). Tolkien also cites Boethius in the *unpublished* draft of the lecture on *Beowulf* (cf. Drout 2002:49).
5 Numerous communications from Shippey to me. See also Shippey (2005:334).
6 See Shippey's critical comment regarding G.E. Moore, the father of English analytical philosophy, in Shippey (2000:158), and also a personal comment regarding a dispute with the Oxford "philosophers" (E-mail 14 July 2009).

many of the ancient Northern texts in which Tolkien took deepest interest (such as *Beowulf*) were simply inscrutable. To understand them at all, let alone edit them, comparative philologists first had to compose grammars of extinct languages for which (unlike Latin and Greek) there was no living tradition. They did this, essentially, by working out the processes of mostly phonetic change which had created the languages, and so marked off, for instance, Old English and Old Norse from their Common Germanic stem. But this involved working out the grammar and phonology of Common Germanic, of which almost nothing had ever been recorded. Only then could editors begin to refine their knowledge, understand, edit and even emend texts (as Tolkien did, for instance in his posthumously-published edition *The Old English Exodus: Text, Translation and Commentary*) which had been poorly transmitted. And only after that could they start to understand poems, names, legends, myths.

I have commented on this historical process elsewhere,[7] but the most important conclusions I would draw are these. First, comparative philology is about linguistic *change*. This interest is reflected in the enormous effort Tolkien put into his linguistic sub-creations, not only inventing his elvish languages, but showing how Sindarin, for instance, had developed out of Quenya. Second, comparative philology, focused on change as it was, gave deep and unexpected insights into history. Language and history, or language and legend, were not to be kept separate from each other. Third – especially important in Tolkien's professional life – the traditional disciplinary separation of "language" and "literature" within British university departments was entirely mistaken (*Letters* no. 7). Finally, it should never be forgotten that to Tolkien comparative philology was still a new discipline, not well understood, with few defenders.

All this may tell us why Tolkien rarely mentioned philosophers. For one thing, philosophy and old-style philology were often seen as opposed. To the philosopher, the old-style philologist – the lover of words, the lover of literature – seemed what we might call a pedant, concerned with tricks of style, with purity of expression, never going below the surface of human speech and writing to the deeper truths that lay beneath. Harmless, one might say,

---

7 Shippey (2005: chs. 1-2). These chapters are however little changed from the first edition of 1982.

but trivial. Tolkien would certainly reply that even if that had been true of old-style Classical philology, it was completely untrue of the new-style *comparative* philology which had been born in the 19th century: for this entirely new discipline, of which Plato and Aristotle and Thomas Aquinas knew nothing, had opened up completely new perspectives on the nature of language, and the nature of history, and the nature of mythology, even the nature of humanity. What philologists like Jacob Grimm had shown was how language changed over time – which among other things showed how languages, and peoples, are related. And the techniques they developed were extraordinarily rigorous: my old professor once told me that mastering the sound-changes of comparative Germanic philology was the hardest intellectual work he ever did, and he was a man who had bought and read his own copy of the sixty-volume edition of Aquinas's *Summa Theologiae*.

Let me give one example, out of many millions that are possible. The Italian word for the number "five" is *cinque*, while the English word is "five". The two words do not sound anything like each other. They do not share a single sound! And yet we can show how they are related.

- The Italian word descends from Latin *quinque*
- but in Latin the *qu-* sound corresponds exactly to *p-* in other ancient Italian languages, such as Oscan and Umbrian, where the word would be *pempe*
- we find just this alternation of *qu-* and *p-* also in the Celtic languages, so that the Irish word for "five" is *coig* (pronounced "queeg"), but the Welsh is *pimp*
- the ancestor of Latin and Oscan, then, may have had a word like *pinpe*
- but in Germanic languages, that ancient *p-* regularly becomes *f-*, so that Latin *pater* is German *Vater* (pronounced with an initial *f-*)
- which is why our ancient ancestral *pinpe* became German *fünf*
- but one of the peculiarities of English is that in it, unlike other Germanic languages, a short vowel is lengthened before a nasal sound, and the nasal sound is dropped, so that we have Old English *fíf* (and note that much the same has happened with Irish *coig*)
- finally, two sound-changes, one occurring (unlike all the others) during the period of recorded history, and the other still operative to this day, the vowel *i* has become *ai*, and the final *-f* has become a *-v*.

And that is why *cinque* and "five" are the same word!

Now, you can see why philologists are thought to be pedantic! What I have said is very detailed, and it doesn't seem to mean anything. But it tells us a lot about history, or prehistory, such as the way in which languages are related. Philology – and again I mean *comparative* philology – is like language DNA-analysis. It had the same effect on the humanities in the 19th century that Darwin had on the biological sciences. And the changes it tracks (like DNA-analysis) are not under conscious control. No-one ever designed them, and though similar processes are still at work even today, we are rarely conscious of them, because they happen so slowly, and we do not know what causes them. You might say that phonological changes may tell us a great deal, but in themselves they do not *mean* anything. There is no philosophy in them.

Not surprisingly, therefore, philosophers do not think the same way as philologists. I will give you one example. Many years ago I was interviewing candidates for an important university scholarship, and one candidate was said to be the best philosopher of his year at the University of Oxford. He told us that he was studying the concept of "God" in Augustine, and that he was focusing on the difference in Augustine's writings between "a god" and "the god" and "God". I thought about this for a minute or two, and then asked, "but Augustine wrote in Latin, which has neither a definite nor an indefinite article. So how can you tell whether he meant 'the god' or 'God' or 'a god' when he wrote *deus*?" The brilliant young philosopher gaped at me. He had not thought of that (I expect he was working from an English translation). He did not get the scholarship, and all the philosophers were very angry with me, but what could I say? I am a philologist. I know very little of concepts of god, and I do not presume to say what Augustine may have *meant* by *deus*, but I do know something about grammar.

And there is a difference of temperament as well. It was the philosopher William James who pointed this out.[8] We all, he wrote, have two impulses in us, but we have them in different proportions. One is the impulse to generalise, to organise facts into systems and patterns, to see how things are connected. The other is to look at details, at specifics, to see how things are different. They should of course be balanced, but I would suggest that philosophers are the generalisers, the ones with the telescope. Philologists are the scrutinisers, the ones with the

---

8 Shippey (2005:380-82 and note on 448).

microscope. Tolkien was a very extreme example of the latter. He himself noted that his intellectual fault was the tendency to "niggle" – to waste time and effort on unnecessary detail.[9] That is why he never finished the *Silmarillion*, despite working on it for nearly sixty years. So that is one reason for Tolkien not to mention philosophy or philosophers: because he was a philologist.

The other reason is this. Philosophy is too important to be left to philosophers. Philosophy deals with the great questions of human life, and anyone who has lived for very long is at least aware of them. Why must we die? Why are our lives so different from each other? Is there no justice in the world? Are we merely the victims of chance? Anyone who has asked any of these questions – and surely that means all of us – is beginning to be a philosopher. And we all develop our own answers, our own personal philosophy. We may not be able to put it into words, and our personal philosophies may not be as powerful, as thoughtful, as wide-ranging as those of Plato or Boethius, but we are all philosophers of a kind.

Now, in our time, academic philosophers have ceased to have much to do with ordinary people. They do not talk the same language, and the language of academic philosophers is more and more impenetrable. So are ordinary people to be left to their own thought? To construct, as Kurt Vonnegut said cruelly but truthfully in his 1963 novel *Cat's Cradle*, a philosophy of life out of bumper-stickers? It was one aim of the Inklings, I believe, and especially of Tolkien's great friend C.S. Lewis, to bridge this gap. We might note, incidentally, that Lewis had completed the Oxford Classics course, "Greats", which had in it a large element of philosophy, whereas Tolkien did rather badly in his first Oxford examination in this course (despite an alpha in his one paper on Comparative Philology), and at that point, in 1913, abandoned the Oxford Classics course and began to read the then-unfashionable subject of English instead (Carpenter 2000:70-71). Nevertheless, I think even Lewis would agree that we do not need to know the history of philosophy to be philosophers.

So those are my two explanations for Tolkien's reluctance to mention philosophy and philosophers. He was a philologist. And his philosophy was personal.

---

9 In a letter to his publisher, Rayner Unwin, he wrote "I am a natural niggler, alas!" (*Letters* no. 236). It is clear that the painter Niggle who cannot finish his great work is a self-image of Tolkien – see his short story "Leaf by Niggle", and my comments on it (Shippey 2000:266-77).

2. The possible influence of philosophical ideas on Tolkien's works

Franco Manni

I would like to list briefly the ideas of ancient and medieval philosophers that are present in Tolkien's works.

Plato:[10] the use of myths to illustrate ideas; light described in the *Silmarillion* as the Sun (symbol of the Idea of Good) as in the *Republic*; the use of the term "demiurgic" from Plato's *Timaeus*; the Isle of Númenor from Plato's story of Atlantis in *Critias*; the One Ring from that of Gyges, again in the *Republic*; the Elves' reincarnation from *Phaedo*; the idea expressed in *Gorgias* ("it is better to suffer an injustice than to perpetrate it") is the basis of Tolkien's idea on the use of the One Ring, namely that it is better to suffer not using it than to obtain victory by using it; the problematic mind/body dualism in the *Athrabeth* compares the ideas of Plato, Aristotle and several biblical authors.

Augustine: against Manichaeism, the idea that God created everything and Evil is not a fundamental principle; against Pelagianism, the idea that predestination and grace make obedience to divine will unnecessary.

Boethius:[11] divine omniscience does not determine future events;[12] that "consolation" is one of the benefits of reading fables; the notions of "chance" and "luck" do not exist because "providence" does; the followers of Evil will come to nothing because it is only "privation"; the idea, derived in turn from *Gorgias*, that the wicked follow their desires but do not obtain their wishes, which explains the differing purposes and achievements of Gandalf and Saruman; the idea (also taken from *Gorgias*) that a punished evildoer is more fortunate than he who escapes punishment, illustrated by episodes concerning Melkor, Sauron, Boromir and Gollum.

Thomas Aquinas: in Note 8 to the comment that Tolkien made on *Athrabeth* he discusses "desire" and distinguishes three types: "natural" desire which is

---

10 It should be remembered that in 1913 Tolkien sat an examination on two dialogues from *Gorgias*, *Phaedo* and *Protagoras* (Hammond & Scull 2006:37).
11 In 1915 Tolkien sat an examination on *De consolatione philosophiae* (Hammond & Scull 2006:39).
12 Cf. Note 6 to *Ósanwe-kenta* in *LTP* 21-22.

common to all members of a species, "personal" desire which concerns one's individual situation, and "illusionary" desire, which obstructs the understanding that things are not as they should be and leads to the delusion that they are as one would wish them to be (*MR* 343). This distinction is the same made by Thomas Aquinas in an article[13] in *Summa Theologiae*, a work which Carpenter says was present on Lewis's bookshelf during the Inklings evening meetings (Carpenter 1978:128) and which Claudio Testi tells me that he knows Tolkien to have possessed.[14]

Another undeclared Thomistic point: the difference between the two kinds of Hope, *Admir* and *Estel*, which Andreth distinguishes in *Athrabeth* (*MR* 320) is similar to the distinction made in *Summa Theologiae* between *spes* as a pre-moral feeling present also in drunk people and brute animals and whose object is "a difficult, but possible, future good",[15] and *spes* as a theological virtue, of which he writes:

> Hope does not trust chiefly in grace already received, but on God's omnipotence and mercy, whereby even he that has not grace, can obtain it, so as to come to eternal life. Now whoever has faith is certain of God's omnipotence and mercy. [...] That some who have hope fail to obtain happiness, is due to a fault of the free will in placing the obstacle of sin, but not to any deficiency in God's power or mercy, in which hope places its trust. Hence this does not prejudice the certainty of hope.[16]

There are also Tolkenian links with the ideas of several modern philosophers.

E.F. Carritt, Collingwood's philosophy tutor, in his 1914 *Theory of Beauty* (Carritt 1914:98) discusses Addison's ideas on the creative imagination and

---

13 *Summa Theologiae, Pars prima secundae*, q. 34, art. 2. Aquinas distinguishes three kinds of "pleasure" ("pleasure" is the feeling which follows a fulfilled desire of a "good thing" [*bonum*]) based on three kinds of *bonum*: a) *bonum per se*, i.e. *per suam naturam* and thus universal; b) *bonum conveniens secundum dispositionem* not universal, but associated with some "not natural" circumstances, for example some plants are medicines for an ill man although poisonous for healthy men; c) *apparens bonum*, when a man wrongly thinks good what is actually evil. For me the parallels between Tolkien's "natural desire" and Aquinas's *bonum per se*, Tolkien's "personal desire" and Aquinas's *bonum conveniens secundum dispositionem*, and Tolkien's "illusionary desire" and Aquinas's *apparens bonum* are evident.
14 Claudio Testi has purchased a copy owned and signed by Tolkien on the collectors' market; the authenticity of the handwriting was confirmed by Verlyn Flieger and, via Carl Hostetter, by Christopher Tolkien.
15 *Summa Theologiae, Pars prima secundae*, q. 40, art. 1, 3, 6.
16 *Summa Theologiae, Pars secunda secundae*, q. 18, art. 4, *ad secundum et ad tertium*. On Aquinas as a source for Tolkien see Birzer 2007.

its "secret satisfactions". Carritt also mentions ideas of Schopenhauer: music gives us the *Universalia ante rem* (the Music of the Ainur which precedes the shaping of Arda); art as "escapism"; art as "refreshment"; the different (positive and negative) meanings of fantasy and imagination.[17]

Chris Seeman, on the other hand, thinks that Tolkien took the ideas of "secondary belief" and "imagination/fantasy" from Coleridge.[18]

Describing Oxford in the 1920s, Fred Inglis wrote that, unlike other lecturers – who might be lazy, negligent dandies – the philosophers (Cook Wilson, J.A. Smith, Harold Joachim, E.F. Carritt) took their lessons and publications more seriously and were more active in discussion societies (Inglis 2009:126): in this respect they seem to resemble the Inklings.

Tolkien would certainly have known the philosopher Robin Collingwood,[19] whose central idea is that of "re-enactment", the re-living of the deeds and thoughts of people from the past; not in "dream-states" as Tolkien had suggested in his two unfinished "time-travel" novels, albeit consciously and rationally:[20] here Aragorn and Arwen re-live the stories of Beren and Lúthien, but make their own judgements on and creative additions to them.

What do you think, Tom, about the presence of some of these philosophical "debts" in Tolkien's works, or others I have not mentioned?

---

17 Schopenhauer, Arthur, *The World as Will and Idea*, 1819. III, § 52 (references from Carritt's book).
18 Seeman (1995:74).
19 For references of scholars to relations between Tolkien and Collingwood, see Manni (2012:25-26) and see also A. Lewis (2009:15). In his work *The Philosophy of Enchantment* (subtitled *Studies in Folktales, Cultural Criticism, and Anthropology*), written during the years in which Tolkien was preparing his lecture "On Fairy-stories", Collingwood dealt with topics that were also studied by Tolkien; the historical and geographical spread of fables, their relation to human archetypes and function for both adults and children.
20 "Thought can never be mere object. To know someone else's activity of thinking is possible only on the assumption that this same activity can be re-enacted in one's own mind. In that sense, to know what someone is thinking (or has thought) involves thinking it for oneself. [...] And this does not appear a satisfactory account of historical thought only to persons who embrace the fundamental error of mistaking for history that form of pseudo-history which Croce has called 'philological history': persons who think that history is nothing more than scholarship or learning, and would assign to the historian the self-contradictory task of discovering (for example) 'what Plato thought' without inquiring 'whether it is true'." (Collingwood 1992:215-16, 287, 300).

Tom Shippey

Here I would like to say a few words about only three of the philosophers mentioned by Franco: Plato, the pagan; Boethius, the Catholic Christian who (like Tolkien) avoids all mention of Christianity in his most famous work; and Robin Collingwood, Tolkien's colleague at Pembroke College, Oxford.

To take Plato first: my friend Professor Hutton has pointed out that the distinguishing feature of neo-Platonism is the belief in demiurges, superhuman or angelic powers subordinate to God but taking a major part in directing human affairs.[21] What this belief offered was a way of connecting and harmonising pagan Classical tradition with Christian belief. It has become very clear that Tolkien's close friend Lewis was a modern neo-Platonist. In his cosmology the pagan gods Mars, Venus, Mercury, Jupiter, Saturn have become the presiding spirits, or eldils, of their respective planets, while the presiding spirit of this planet, Earth, is the "bent eldil", Satan, *princeps huius mundi*, the prince of this world.[22] So the Classical pagan religion had a basis of truth, but had been misunderstood.

I think that Tolkien, long before he met Lewis, had a similar goal, which was to try to integrate the Northern pagan religion with Christianity, which he did – in a way very similar to Lewis's – by making the Valar, the powers of Middle-earth, resemble the description of the Norse gods as given by the Icelander Snorri Sturluson in his *Prose Edda*.[23] So you might say that Tolkien was a Northern neo-Platonist. However, it is possible that as time went by Tolkien became unsure about the propriety of this integration, and started to make his cosmology less like the old Northern one. The Valar interfere very little, if at all, in the action of *The Lord of the Rings*. They have delegated their authority even further to the Maiar and the Istari, like Gandalf.

---

21 Hutton 2003, especially ch. 3, "The New Old Paganism", and ch. 7, "The Inklings and the Gods".
22 See now Michael Ward, *Planet Narnia: The Seven Heavens in the Imagination of C.S. Lewis.*.
23 Most obviously in Tolkien, *Lost Tales I*, 64-93.

Then there is Collingwood: I am astonished at the lack of mention of Collingwood by Tolkien, and vice versa.[24] They must have had lunch together in the Pembroke Common Room on many occasions, both were thinking and writing about fairy-tales at the same time,[25] but I can see no trace of influence either way. This is the more surprising because Tolkien must also have known Collingwood's father, W.G. Collingwood. I do not think I would call W.G. a philologist, but he was a friend to philology: one of the founding members of the Viking Society in England, author of an important work on Northern archaeology, of another book of travels in Iceland, and he also wrote three historical novels set in Anglo-Saxon England, which Tolkien would surely have read. He brought together many of Tolkien's own interests, including – not long before he died in 1932 – a study of the historical campaigns of King Arthur.[26] Robin Collingwood also combined archaeology, history, and fairy-tale, as well as philosophy. Why were the two men not closer together?

I can only make this suggestion, which is that Tolkien was often annoyed by people who shared his interests, but did not see them in quite the same way that he did. He thought Shakespeare had very good ideas in *Macbeth* (with the march of the trees), and in *Midsummer Night's Dream* (where the fairies mislead humans as the elves do in *The Hobbit*): but Shakespeare did not do them *right*! (Carpenter 2000:35) Wagner also in many ways had the same inspirations as Tolkien, in his opera sequence *Der Ring des Nibelungen*: but he got the story *wrong*, and Tolkien had to rewrite it in his *Legend of Sigurd and Gudrún*.[27] Perhaps in the same way

---

24 Actually Collingwood explicitly mentions Tolkien in a text published as appendix to its famous *The Idea of History* (Collingwood 1992:440-41; cf. Noad 2010:11-12) and twice in his work published in 1936, *Roman Britain and the English Settlements* (cf. Hammond & Scull 2006b; Drout 2007a). Tolkien instead mentions Collingwood in the manuscript A14/2 preserved in the Oxford Bodleian Library. In a paper, unfortunately still unpublished, delivered in 2004 at the International Congress on Medieval Studies of the Kalamazoo University, entitled "Tolkien and the Collingwoods: Neo-Medievalism, Theories of the Fairy Tale, and History as Science", Douglas A. Anderson suggested that precisely Collingwood took Tolkien inside the Lidney Park project due to its research on "Nodens" [http://www.wmich.edu/medieval/congress/archive/session-archive.html]. This assumption is supported also by Wayne Hammond and Christina Scull on their blog. Moreover, there are several references to Tolkien in the recent Collingwood biography written by Fred Inglis (Inglis 2009:105): "In 1926 things went slightly better, at least for Collingwood, when J.R.R. Tolkien was elected College member, and both noticed a common passion for philology and folklore."
25 As we now know from Collingwood's posthumously-published *The Philosophy of Enchantment: Studies in Folktale, Cultural Criticism, and Anthropology*.
26 The elder Collingwood is discussed in Andrew Wawn, *The Vikings and the Victorians: Inventing the Old North in Nineteenth century Britain*, especially pp. 335-40.
27 Note the dismissal of Wagner as an influence by Christopher Tolkien in *SG* 10. See however Vink 2012 and MacLachlan 2012.

Tolkien thought Collingwood was a little off target, and even – dare I say it – a little silly. His most famous and influential historical comments are the ones in a volume of the respectable and authoritative "Oxford History of England" in which he argued that perhaps the legends of King Arthur and his knights were true after all (as his father had argued not long before): many years later his collaborator J.N.L. Myres very determinedly dissociated himself from these remarks and had his section of the book revised and reprinted separately.[28] I can imagine Tolkien, too, puffing his pipe as he read those pages, and frowning.

Finally, there is Boethius. We should not forget that, in spite of his world-wide appeal, Tolkien had narrow loyalties, primarily to England, not Great Britain, not the United Kingdom, but England. He was always especially interested in English reactions and traditions. Here I feel sure that the Old English version of Boethius – which in some ways is more than a translation – was of special interest to him. Though the most recent edition of this work[29] casts doubt on the ascription, for more than a thousand years it has been taken to be the work of King Alfred himself, the only English king to be regularly given the title of "the Great", and Tolkien himself almost certainly accepted the traditional view that it gave special insight into the thought of a national hero.

The original work is especially challenging in that Boethius, writing as a prisoner under sentence of death, actually produced a "consolation" for someone unable to take action: and the "consolation" consists of arguments that all is for the best, that what seems evil is an unnoticed good, that we must accept the divine pattern which we ourselves are not equipped to perceive. But the Old English work at times takes a different view, which one can well understand if it is the work of King Alfred himself. Alfred, as king of a kingdom under terrible pressure from a cruel and pagan enemy determined to kill him personally, and his family, and destroy his kingdom, and wipe out his religion, could not afford to be passive and resigned. He had to take action: build forts, recruit armies, win battles, hang prisoners, execute hostages, kill the enemy wounded. The discovery of fifty headless corpses in a pit not far from my home a few weeks ago, corpses identified

---

[28] See Collingwood & Myres (1936:321-24), and Myres 1986. Myres's statement of dissociation from the earlier work is on pages xvi-xvii. Note also Myres's contemptuous dismissal of the whole Arthur issue on page 16.
[29] Godden and Irvine (eds.). 2009. *The Old English Boethius*.

as Scandinavians by the DNA in their teeth, indicates that the Anglo-Saxons did not apply Boethian solutions to their political problems. Nor, of course, did Tolkien's countrymen in the war in which he fought, and the later war in which his son served. I hope to say more about this later on, but here I will just say that King Alfred's Boethius seems to me to be at times more realistic, and of course more English, than Boethius's Boethius. And perhaps also less philosophical, less of a consolation, more of a programme of action.

Lewis said that Tolkien was a man who could not be influenced. He either ignored what you said, or he did everything over again.[30] I would say, very briefly, that he did not engage with philosophers, nor did he argue with them. He tried instead to state things better than they did, though they might be the same things.

3. Philology and Philosophy

Franco Manni

To counter your criticisms of philosophy, Tom, I offer two sets of arguments, one logical and the other historical.

Logical arguments

1) Although a philosopher may be uncultivated and poorly prepared, so might a philologist, an engineer or a lawyer! In your example the young examinee did not know that there is no article in Latin. In particular I would claim that for a philosopher, cultural weakness means a lack of *historical* knowledge (Classical tongues, political history, history of ideas etc.). With respect to your example, it seems to me that it is possible to deduce from their context the different meanings of the word *deus* ("divine nature", "heathen deity" or "Christian God") in Augustine's philosophical works.

2) You say that philosophers have despised philologists as "pedants". I agree that this has often happened, either because of the superficiality of *some* phi-

---

30 Carpenter (2000:149 and further 204), again quoting Lewis, "No one ever influenced Tolkien – you might as well try to influence a bandersnatch."

losophers (of which I too disapprove!), but also because of what I believe to be the illegitimate claims of some philologists: "our digging out and collecting of erudite details is sufficient to build the history of any human matter." The arrogance of such claims was well described by Benedetto Croce (Croce 2001: 31) – who prized philology highly! – and criticised by Tolkien in his lecture on *Beowulf*, and by you in *Roots and Branches* (Shippey 2007:85-87) in a discussion of the weaknesses of Jacob Grimm's *Teutonic Mythology*.

3) You assert that philosophers generalise, whereas philologists care about details. This seems to me too simplistic. On one hand many philosophers immerse themselves in a veritable forest of detailed distinctions (for example Aristotle's writings on logic, such as *Prior Analytics, Posterior Analytics* etc.); on the other hand, philologists too generalise, speculate and theorise, both in textual criticism and linguistics, as I shall try to demonstrate in my "Historical argument" below.

4) In your example regarding the Latin word *quinque*, you seem to suggest that there is just one kind of knowledge, a sort of epistemological reductionism! But to me it appears obvious that philosophy of language *does not* substitute phonetics, and Aristotle's or Rawls's ethical reflections on justice *do not* substitute the government's calculations of house taxes and Hegel's dialectics *do not* substitute S.J. Gould's analysis of the genetic variation of Caribbean molluscs (even though Gould reflected on and admired Hegelian dialectics).

5) You suggest that philosophy is too important to be left to philosophers. I agree that many "philosophers" are narrow-minded and have little influence on thought in general (nevertheless most politicians are not Cromwell, and most chemists are not Lavoisier!), but do you really think that the thoughts of Aristotle, Augustine, Machiavelli, Voltaire, Adam Smith, Freud and Marx left unchanged the thoughts of the "common man"? That those theories have not influenced him, directly or indirectly? Or that a lone individual, reflecting on the events of his life, has the capacity to conceive ideas such as human rights, the evolution of species, the separation of powers, the objections to Manichaeism, the free market, the development of sexuality, and so on? I think that – although it is certainly not necessary to have read original philosophical texts – in order to philosophize *well* one needs ideas that derive from (great) philosophers.

6) You wrote that there is no science of "comparative mythology" capable of producing results on a par with those of comparative philology. I think that is because philology alone is insufficient for the historical comprehension of human culture and values. And the same is true of philosophy. As Vico said: philology is blind without philosophy, and philosophy empty without philology. Both are incapable of becoming history. I think that your underestimation of philosophy arises from not bearing in mind that philosophical tradition which more or less began with Vico and developed during the 19th and 20th centuries, sometimes known as historicism: *philologia et philosophia geminae hortae!*[31]

Historical arguments

Many eminent philologists were in fact influenced by philosophers, and it is probable that Tolkien – unlikely to have been an isolated rarity in the philological tradition – was also directly or indirectly affected via the writings of great philologists which he knew well, whether or not he made this explicit.

The Classical philologist Ulrich von Wilamowitz wrote that Vico and the ideas of the philosopher Herder inspired his interest in the history of peoples and unconscious, collective artistic creation, and that only after this was he able to understand legends: without these philosophers comparative linguistics would have been impossible. In particular, Wilamowitz cites the influence of Kant on the philologist G. Hermann and of the philosopher W. von Humboldt on the philologist Bekker's textual criticism (von Wilamowitz 1967:92, 96, 104).

The philologist S. Timpanaro writes that the Swiss philologist J.C. Orelli was influenced by the philosopher Pestalozzi (Timpanaro 1963:43).

The Danish philologist Grundtvig (held in high regard by Tolkien) after reading the German philosopher Schelling's essay *Bruno* about the noted 16th century Italian philosopher, wrote "I dared to acknowledge the truth: reality holds no joy for me. I looked for life in his *Bruno*." He also wrote a poem, *Gottlieb Fichte*, addressed to Schelling: "your gigantic voice wakened me from my false tranquillity, wakened me to doubt and belief, reminded me of the light of truth

---

31 Philology and philosophy share a common birth; Croce (1913:29-33) (translation by Robin G. Collingwood, fellow and lecturer at Pembroke College, Oxford).

and the blossoms of love." Grundtvig's interest for Nordic mythology arose from reading the works of the philosopher F. Schlegel.[32]

Croce thought that philosophers and historians came together for the first time in the Romantic movement, giving birth to a new philological school and to works like *Monumenta Germaniae Historica* and *Corpus Inscriptionum Latinarum* (Croce 2001:304-6).

The philologist W.P. Lehmann writes that the philosopher Leibniz studied historical linguistics and helped the philologist J.C. Adelung to find material for his *Mithridates*. Lehmann also writes that in 1808 the philosopher F. Schlegel published *Über die Sprache und die Weisheit der Inder* in which – using comparative anatomy as a model – he sought evidence regarding the genealogy of languages in comparative grammar. Four years after this work, the anatomist G. Cuvier published his popular treatise on comparative anatomy *Recherches sur les ossemens fossiles de quadrupèdes*. Philologist Franz Bopp's 1816 work on the system of conjugation in Sanskrit compared to those of Greek, Latin, Persian and German, *Über das Conjugationssytem der Sanskritsprache in Vergleichung mit jenem der griechischen, lateinischen, persischen und germanischen Sprache*, had no need of further models. Three years after Bopp's book, Jacob Grimm published the first volume of *Deutsche Grammatik* and – after having read the book *Undersøgelse om det gamle Nordiske eller Islandske Sprogs Oprindelse* by philologist R. Rask (1818) – rewrote it, formulating the basic rules of what became historical phonology.[33]

Jacob Grimm would certainly have known Vico through Savigny, who appreciated him and recommended his works to Niebuhr (another of the Grimm brothers' intellectual forebears), and through Herder in Germany, who knew Vico's writings well.[34] The influence of Kant on Grimm's mentor Savigny was

---

32 For quotations in this section, see Bradley (2008:377, 416, 543).
33 Lehmann, *Historical Linguistics: an Introduction*. The philologist William D. Whitney (*La vie du langage*, Paris: Librairie Germer, 1875:261), also thought that the birth of linguistics was brought about by the speculations of philosophers such as Leibniz and Herder.
34 Cf. Marini 1974. The only philosophy Grimm accepted was that useful for understanding history, not the systematic philosophy of Christian Wolff. For thoughts on philosophy in Grimm's works, see Jacob Grimm, *Kleiner Schriften*, Bd. 8, 32-33; Grimm's letter to Savigny, after the latter had published *Vom Beruf unsrer Zeit für Gesetzgebung und Rechtswissenschaft* (in *Briefe der Bruder Grimm an Savigny*, Berlin 1953, 171-78, in particular 173); Grimm's review of Wilhelm Müller's *Geschichte und System der altdeutschen Religion*, which says: "If you want to call this speculative attitude 'philosophical spirit', I would rather philosophize outside of things and not within them" (Marini 1974).

also important (see the studies by Wieacker, Kiefner and Meder).[35] His reception of post-Kantian idealism (Fichte, Fries, Schlegel, Höerderlin) is documented by Rückert (Rückert 1984:232-300) and Nörr.[36] In 1841 Jacob Grimm admitted that his cultural interests had been shaped not so much by the Romantic notion of culture that developed in successive stages, as by the experience of "shame and humiliation" he underwent when his homeland was occupied by a foreign power. In response to this threat to his national identity, he put the historical principle to use not so much to grasp the present as to sum up the past, so as to construct a past that could function as an "invisible umbrella against the enemy's arrogance" (Toews 2004:320). To assert one's own identity, one had to recreate the world in which one's own tongue had attained its first meanings. Jacob Grimm dedicated his *Deutsche Grammatik* to Savigny, because, when his father had died in 1796, he had been taken in as an orphan by Savigny, together with his four brothers and sister, entering into a new world of friendships and family connections (Toews 2004:294, 319, 320, 330). Nevertheless, in 1850 Grimm wrote a theoretical essay influenced by the philosophers Schelling, Schlegel, Herder, Hegel and von Humboldt (Meli 1992:49-50).

Franz Bopp, a German linguist known for extensive work on the origins of Indo-European languages, while at Aschaffenburg, was attracted to oriental languages by the lectures of Karl J. Windischmann – a philosopher influenced by Schelling who was full of enthusiasm for Indian philosophy – and was further stimulated by F. Schlegel's book, *Über die Sprache und Weisheit der Inder* (Heidelberg, 1808).

Concerning the great philologist Karl Lachmann, Germanic, Classical and Biblical scholar, Timpanaro writes that there is a parallel between the *stemmata codicum* of textual criticism and the "genealogical tree" of languages introduced by Schleicher in comparative linguistics (Timpanaro 1963:71). Schleicher thought that phonological changes were corruptions of an original "perfection", analogous to the textual errors that accumulate along the *stemma codicum* of a manuscript-archetype (Timpanaro 1963:71). Lachmann exaggerated in his under-valuation of the *codices recentiores*, much as contemporary

---

35 Cf. Toews 2004.
36 Cf. Nörr 1994.

scholars under-valued the more recent tongues, believing that Sanskrit (being the oldest known tongue) preserved the most ancient and original form of all languages, and was thus the most "perfect" (Timpanaro 1963:74).

One might have thought that textual critics such as Lachmann perhaps took their ideas from comparative linguistics, but the converse is more likely (from textual criticism to comparative linguistics). According to Timpanaro, though, neither hypothesis is correct: Schleicher was inspired by the natural sciences model and not that of classical philology, holding that comparative linguistics was not historical, but rather a *Naturorganismus*! Timpanaro sees a common origin for textual criticism, comparative anatomy in a sort of "comparative mentality" that was widespread in the early 19th century (Timpanaro 1963:76).

The philologist Fiesoli reports that in the Berlin *Dreiftaltigkeitsfriedhof* Lachmann's tomb may be seen next to that of the philosopher Schleiermacher, since before he died Lachmann asked to be buried beside the friend who had been "always close to him during mortal life" (Fiesoli 2000:109, 127, 129). Frequent epistolary exchanges between the two scholars and the laudatory dedication to Schleiermacher in the *Incipit* of Lachmann's *Rechenschaft* are sufficient proof of their reciprocal esteem. Moreover, Lutz-Hensel noted the similarity of the words both used when comparing "good conjectures" with respect to "bad manuscripts".

Schleiermacher, in his *Vorlesungen*, wrote that "philological" criticism coincides with the "historical", because it is necessary first to reconstruct the "fact" (the original document): there are two kinds of philological criticism, and only the second of these is suitable for evaluating a document's level of reliability. He shared Lachmann's diffidence towards *codices recentiores* and rare variants (Fiesoli 2000:133). According to the philosopher, Lachmann had only one final step to take: that of adding critical analysis to hermeneutic analysis. And it was precisely this that Lachmann began to do in his *editio maior* of the New Testament. Here when defining *recensio* and *emendatio*, Lachmann uses a "philosophical" – rather than "philological" – style; he theorizes and shapes "universals". Thus Lachmann closes the hermeneutic circle inspired by Schleiermacher, with a famous distinction between *verum* and *veri simile* (Fiesoli 2000:135).

Philologist M. Olender writes that the Semitic language philologist J.-E. Renan read Herder at Saint-Sulpice and felt as though he were "entering a temple [...] It was exactly what I was looking for, the combination of a highly religious with a critical spirit [...] so that I might be more a philosopher without ceasing to be a Christian." He also writes that the Indo-European philologist Adolphe Pictet in 1820 in Paris became interested in the philosopher V. Cousin and dreamed of founding with him a *Revue Philosophique*. During the winter of 1821-22 Pictet made a philosophical pilgrimage to Germany and met Goethe, Schelling, Schleiermacher and Hegel (Olender 2008:86, 88, 90, 93-4).

A. Schleicher – influenced by Positivist philosophy – tried to shape a Darwinian model for linguistics as a "natural science", but Steinberg wrote[37] that this idea of linguistics as *Naturorganismus* derived from Hegel, the philosophy of whom Schleicher had studied in Bonn and espoused when at Tübingen. Schleicher knew the Darwinian model only indirectly, from the writings of the philosopher H. Spencer, who had in fact published his idea of the evolution of species before Darwin and Wallace; but Spencer at that time – as Lamarck – believed in the inheritance of acquired characteristics rather than natural selection.

The Germanic philologist W.P. Ker – much esteemed by Tolkien – in his *Epic and Romance* (1896) discussed at length (for tens of pages) the *Poetics* of the philosopher Aristotle.

H.U. Gumbrecht writes that the philologist Wilamowitz was under the influence of the philosopher Herder's writings, and that his disciple, philologist W. Jaeger, "saw a decisive potential for the renovation of Classical philology in the writings of Nietzsche and Dilthey" (Gumbrecht 2003:51).

Lachmann's method suffered a crisis in the late 19th century when Wilamowitz realized that it could not be applied mechanically: tradition is complex, the scholar needs to know the "culture" of Antiquity and the Middle Ages and pay attention to "internal" criteria (*lectio difficilior, usus scribendi*). Even the most suspect *codex* might harbour a correct variant. Meanwhile, comparative linguistics also experienced a crisis: J. Schmidt and P. Kretschener (Germanic philologists) and H. Schuchardt (a Romance philologist) proposed a "horizontal

---

37 *Indogermanische Forschungen*, vol. VII, Berlin: Walter de Gruyter, 1897, 360 and followings.

theory": kinship between tongues occurs through reciprocal influences and not genealogical descent. Much as in the 1850s and 60s scholars of languages and textual critics had breathed a common evolutionist and comparative air, so at the end of the 19th century they both began to breathe a different air: the reaction against Positivist philosophy. This gave more importance to the study of the origins of Romance – and even living – languages and modified the proposed kinship relations between the Indo-European tongues (Timpanaro 1963:79-83, 87).

The philologist G. Nencioni writes (Nencioni 1989:65-67) that this reaction against Positivism by the philosophers Rickert, Dilthey, Windelband, Bergson, Simmel and Bradley influenced linguistics as well; more importance came to be given to individual linguistic creativity and logical faculties – as may be seen in the work of Schuchardt and Gillieron. They argue against the concept of "regularity" in phonetic change and the "collectivity" of linguistic inspiration; for them each word has its own life, both semantic and phonetic; they criticize the concept of "idiomatic unity" and emphasize the individuality of each linguistic datum. For Gillieron the word is the focus of linguistic investigation (see e.g. his *Scier dans la Gaule romane*).

In 1922 Benedetto Croce – in a review of work by one of his followers, German philologist Karl Vossler – spoke of a crisis in linguistics: in the mid-19th century the "phonological law" had been considered a "natural law", whereas it had come to be understood by scholars in the field as "scientific" and "abstract", revealing its limits in the field of etymology, that is in the face of real "historical" problems (Nencioni 1989:72).

In his *Individualismus* (1923, *Festschrift für W. Streitberg*) H. Schuchardt referred to himself as "an idealist" like Vossler, agreeing with Croce's theory that language is an "aesthetic expression", but adding that it is above all "communication" (Nencioni 1989:17). Schuchardt saw these two views not as contradicting one another, but as being complementary: "expression" comes first, but we have language only if there is "communication". If there were just "expression" – as Vossler and Croce said – all grammatical changes would be due to individual speakers, whereas they are almost always produced by the linguistic community (Nencioni 1989:36).

Philologist W. von Wartburg in *Einführung in Problematik und Methodik der Sprachhwissenschaft* (Halle, 1943) wrote that Vossler always tended to treat language as "expression", that is as Saussure's "parole", seeing only what is new, without being able to determine the relationships between the new and the old (Nencioni 1989:37).

Now, Tom, I ask what you think of these arguments of mine.

Tom Shippey

Let me summarise what we have said so far. Franco has asked why I think Tolkien avoided mentioning philosophers or philosophy in his works. And I replied, first, because he was a philologist, and second, because his philosophy was personal, not derived from authority. Franco then asked what I thought of some philosophers Tolkien certainly knew, or knew about, and I responded with reference to Plato and Boethius, and his Oxford colleague Collingwood.

Franco now points out that, historically, philosophers and philologists have often worked together; and, logically, no-one begins from absolutely nothing. The influence of philosophy on all of us is cumulative. So I will take these points up, and begin with Franco's historical argument.

There is no doubt that many of the philologists whom Tolkien respected were influenced by philosophers of their time, whom they often mentioned. But the problem we are discussing is that Tolkien *did not do so*. Was his situation, then, different from that of Grimm or Grundtvig, and the many early philologists mentioned by Franco? I would suggest that it was, and for a reason interestingly if provocatively put by Tolkien's friend C.S. Lewis. In his strongly neo-Platonist work of fiction, *That Hideous Strength* (1945), Lewis introduces a character called Dr Dimble, an academic, who seems to be used in the work largely as a vehicle for putting forward Lewis's own opinions. One thing Dimble says is this:

> Have you ever noticed [...] that the universe, and every little bit of the universe, is always hardening and narrowing and coming to a point? [...] If you dip into any college, or school [...] at a given point in its history you always find that there was a time before that point when there was more elbow-room and contrasts weren't quite so sharp [...] Everything is getting more itself and

more different from everything else all the time [...] Even in literature, poetry and prose draw further and further apart. (Lewis 1945:349-50)

I would suggest that there certainly has been a process of increasing academic specialisation. Someone like Grimm could hope to be, as he was, a kind of polymath, interested in many things. But there was no way you could study them all in a British university in Tolkien's time: the syllabus would not allow it. Tolkien could not avoid the constraints, and the narrowings, of his professional life.

Now, as I have said already in my first response, Tolkien did his very best to broaden the whole concept of philology, but for the most part his arguments fell on deaf ears. Narrow specialisation was the dominant academic practice of his time. There was no place for philosophy in the Oxford English Studies syllabus. As Tolkien's successor in his Leeds Chair I can tell you, with absolute conviction, that there was very little place for philology or language studies either, which were continually under threat from the literary colleagues. Both Tolkien and I had to fight desperately to preserve a little of the philological tradition. Trying to make room for philosophy as well... No. An impossibility. Grimm or Grundtvig were very much freer agents than Tolkien or myself. I do not think one can generalise from them to him.

Franco's logical argument, I think, is a more productive one. None of us have minds which are entirely self-educated. There is always a residue, second-hand, fourth-hand, twentieth-hand, it may be, of previous thought – which of course is hard to pick out and analyse. We ourselves are not aware of it. Two good examples from the list given by Franco are surely Freud and Marx. For every person alive now who has read anything by Freud or Marx, there must be ten thousand who have some awareness of their theories. Tolkien, I am sure, would have strongly rejected both thinkers – but you cannot consciously reject something without being aware of it. Tolkien was certainly aware of and reacting against Marx, though as far as I know he never mentions him: his image of the society of the Shire is one entirely without class-warfare, though not at all without class, from the aristocratic Tooks and Brandybucks to the bourgeois

Bagginses to the proletarian Gamgees.[38] This is one reason why sub-Marxist modern critics have despised Tolkien so much.

As for the older philosophers mentioned by Franco, I am less sure how much of their thought has passed on to modern times. It was one of the achievements of Lewis, in particular, to resurrect Plato and the neo-Platonists and pass on their thought, in fictional terms adapted to a juvenile audience, in his "Narnia" sequence. Are Augustine and Aquinas still at work in the modern world? I do not know. But there is one question left unanswered, and an image Tolkien himself used which may be helpful.

The question is, whether we need to explore the thought of old philosophers to become philosophers ourselves? They did not know some of the things that we know. Their circumstances were not ours. I note with interest Grimm's statement, quoted by Franco, that "what had shaped [Grimm's] own sense of cultural calling was not so much the early Romantic notion of culture developing in progressive stages, but the experience of 'shame and humiliation' produced by his homeland's occupation by a foreign power." It seems to me that Tolkien was, for instance, very interested in the thought of Boethius; but even *more* interested in adapting that thought to his own circumstances, which were shaped by two World Wars, in one of which he fought, and in which 254 of his schoolfellows were killed, while the other was taking place as he wrote *The Lord of the Rings*. How would Boethius have coped with Hitler? Not, I think, very well. In short, there must always be a dialogue *between one's own* experience, and the assertions of authority. Both sides of the dialogue require study.

As for the image I mentioned, it is the famous one of the soup, and the bones of the ox from which the soup has been boiled. Tolkien said, very firmly, that

---

38 National solidarity, as opposed to international class-warfare, was very much an issue in Britain after the First World War and the Russian Revolution of 1917. One author whom Tolkien liked and respected was John Buchan. Marjorie Burns suggests that his novel *Huntingtower* (1921), has close similarities with *The Hobbit* and was a likely source for it, see Burns 2007. I agree, but would add that it is a tale in which Russian and English aristocrats combine with the archetypal bourgeois Dickson McCunn (a grocer, as the dwarves rudely call Bilbo), and with a gang of children from the slums of Glasgow, to foil a Bolshevik plot. One of the running jokes in the story is that the slum children have attended Communist Sunday schools, without understanding their philosophy or even their vocabulary. One of them sings a song about class-consciousness and the defeat of the "Boorjoyzee", but when asked what "boorjoyzee" means, says, "Jaikie thought it was some kind of a draigon" [*sic*]. See further Hooker 2011.

we should be content with the soup and not demand to see the bones of the ox (*MC* 120). He was rejecting the utility of source-study, and as he often did, overstating his case to make a point. I think source-study can be useful, and that philosophers were no doubt among Tolkien's sources. But Tolkien was right in that it is very difficult to analyse soup into its component parts. And I'd add that what is really important is not just the components but the boiling! I mean, the way those intellectual influences are combined afresh in the individual mind. It is rarely possible for any of us to give a full account of what has made us think the way we do, and faint or even forgotten influences from Aristotle or Aquinas may indeed have been present in Tolkien's mind. But the interesting thing, for us, is how he recombined them.

4. On Tolkien's personality

Franco Manni

I will now present a sort of *ad hominem* argument, that is more directly focussed on Tolkien.

1. You say that Tolkien lived in circumstances different from those of 19th century philologists and I agree: everything had changed. The academic world too had changed, as you emphasize quoting Lewis's Mr. Dimble, because of increasing specialisation. The thoughts and hopes of the philologists had also changed, as you wrote in *Roots and Branches* (Shippey 2007:79-96, 115-38, 139-56) since: a) nationalistic purpose declined after the Hitlerian climax, b) illusions of reconstructing lost languages, texts and worlds had been abandoned because too few documents remain, c) there had been a "long defeat" of philological studies in university humanities departments.

2. My research has led me to the conclusion that Tolkien was not significantly influenced by the philosophers of his times: neither the Oxford Idealists (J.A. Smith, E.F. Carritt, F.H. Bradley, H.H. Joachim, B. Bosanquet),[39] nor the

---

[39] But *maybe* Tolkien knew of Croce's *Aesthetics* via Collingwood and Lewis (both of whom knew it well). In his criticism of Chambers, Tolkien opposes the theory of "literary genres" just as Croce did (see Drout 2002:90, 107, 109). *Maybe* Tolkien also knew of Croce and Collingwood's theory of "re-enactment" since he was acquainted with the latter.

Oxbridge Realists and Logical Positivists (B. Russell, G.E. Moore, L. Wittgenstein, G. Ryle, A.J. Ayer).[40] I agree with you when you say that, not having attended the philosophy part of the Oxford Classics course, unlike Lewis, he perhaps felt professionally ill-equipped – "maybe he felt that that was Lewis's business" or "he may [...] have not wished to engage in any kind of argument with them, since he had not had any training in philosophy."

3. According to Lewis, as you remarked recently, Tolkien was a man who was immune against any forms of influence; but Lewis also said that in response to criticism Tolkien was capable of rewriting everything from scratch, and this is being influenced. It is well known that he discarded the "Epilogue" to *The Lord of the Rings* because it had been criticized. You say with regard to Collingwood, on the other hand, that Tolkien was annoyed by people who shared his interests, but did not see them in quite the same way that he did. Yourself in *Roots and Branches* documented a lot of direct Wagnerian influences on Tolkien,[41] even if the moral evaluation of those ideas was absolutely different. And yet he refused to recognize such influences, even erasing references such as in the examples I have cited of Boethius and Jung.[42] Why?

4. It may simply be a question of personality, but what was Tolkien's personality like? I will try to give some answers, while focusing on our topic: philosophy and philology.

4.1 *Tolkien was an orphan*: above you referred to the differences with respect to 19th century philologists; I make the suggestion that the conception of history of Jacob Grimm (himself an orphan) was similar to that of Tolkien: not an optimistic Hegelian conception, but an attempt to reconstruct a lost world. As noted by Toews: Grimm experienced his vocation as a tension with a buried world of the past; for him, to go home meant living in an imagined foreign and enigmatic world that had to be recreated from fragments and remains. Grimm thought that those

---

40 These philosophers were opposed also by Lewis: "there are fewer communists at Cambridge and even the so-called Logical Positivists have less power than at Oxford", from a letter to Don Giovanni Calabria, Dec 5 1954 (Hooper 2007); "do not imagine that the Logical Positivist menace is over. To me it seems that the apologetic position has never in my life been worse than it is now. At the Socratic the enemy often wipe the floor with us. *Quousque domine?*" Letter to Don Bede Griffiths, 22 April 1954 (Hooper 2007).
41 See also MacLachlan 2012 and Vink 2012.
42 See Note 4 above.

in the present could make contact with the buried origins of their own existence through recognition of the radical otherness of the past (Toews 2004:322-23). I believe that Tolkien, too, shared this idea, but that he also had another access to the past, namely that of Hegel, Croce and Collingwood which we may call "re-enactment": the past is not lost, there is no radical otherness with respect to the present; the present in fact keeps the past alive and develops and improves it, giving it meaning. An analysis of Grimm's notion tells us that the core of one's identity, the authentic self, is not conserved, but lost! I suggest that this philosophy (might we call it the temptation of a "philosophizing orphan"?) was present in Tolkien, but was not – at least in his maturity – the prevailing one. That which, in the end, prevailed was, I think, that of "re-enactment".

4.2 *Tolkien was a nationalist.* You wrote me that:

> Tolkien's conviction that English tradition had been slighted, marginalized, and largely lost, is no more than the truth... as for not naming philosophers he did read and know, Boethius, Plato etc., well, maybe this is part of his anti-Classical bias. We know that Tolkien read Latin very well and Greek quite well, but he rarely mentions these either, though when you look, the connections are often quite clear. But Tolkien always felt he was a spokesman for the neglected *native* tradition – not that England produced any early native philosophers, other than King Alfred as an interpreter of Boethius. (E-mail 21 August 2009).

Tolkien himself wrote: "Grundtvig's emendations [to the *Beowulf* poem] seemed almost like sorcery to those unable to swallow the notion that other languages than Latin and Greek and Hebrew had any shape or rules" (Drout 2002:9). Drout cites both Tolkien's conviction that he was the descendant of a Mercian family and yours that Tolkien was able to understand *Beowulf* so well because he was "native" to both tongue and land, but Drout adds that Tolkien would have replied that, if he could understand the poem, this was because he had inherited an enormous amount of previous critical scholarship, and had tried to read it with an open heart and mind, trying to comprehend its intrinsic purpose, rather than comparing it to other works (Drout 2002:9). But why, I wonder, did Tolkien have a mentality so different from that of previous scholars? Might this in part have been due to the cultural changes of the preceding decades? I mean a really new mentality, the same which led Croce and Collingwood to state their theory of historical "re-enactment", a sort of conscious reincarnation, mediated not just by "blood and land", but also through the enormous amount of "previous philological scholarship". Otherwise, quoting Drout again, this "identification across the centuries would rely on the recognition (or, if you prefer, the illusion) of fundamental continuities between one time and another [...] those of masculine, same-sex, non-biological reproduction of identities" (Drout 2002:22). Perhaps a necessary acknowledgement, but I think insufficient: "re-enactment" requires not just a native heritage of blood and land, but also a contribution from the intellect, of ideas. For instance, when you say that "King Alfred's Boethius seems to me to be more realistic, and of course more English, than Boethius's Boethius," I agree, but would add that without Boethius's Boethius, Alfred's could not have existed.

4.3 *Tolkien was a philologist*; I would like to go into more detail.

4.3.1 *Tolkien was a Germanic, not a Classical philologist.* He wrote: "Greek Gods are timeless and do not know or fear death. Such beliefs may hold promise of a profounder thought, so that the Greeks could make philosophy, but the Germanic North created specially the hero" (Drout 2002:128). So Tolkien – as a scholar of *Germanistik* – could more easily focus upon, and occupy himself for decades with heroism rather than philosophy, e.g. by going about his daily tasks of looking up bibliographical references, quotations, etc.

4.3.2 *Tolkien was a Christian philologist and member of the Inklings.* He had to defend his point of view both against academic colleagues and literary critics, two categories that were often Modernist in their poetry and atheist in their philosophy. His friend C.S. Lewis wrote (in criticism of the "culturalist" critical line of Croce, Carritt and Arnold) that: "culture is the storehouse of the best sub-Christian values."[43] Tolkien was a Christian philologist, when most philosophers of the time were atheists, and his mode of defence (different from that of Lewis) seems to have been to avoid surrendering to the enemy by not naming him. How otherwise can we explain the fact that he cited the mediocre Dawson (*OFS* 124:150) rather than the more original Spengler and Toynbee?[44] All three were philosophers of history, but only the first a committed Christian.

---

43 Letter to his brother Warnie, 28 April 1940 (Hooper 2004).
44 "I don't know of any direct evidence, but I would be shocked if he didn't know something about Spengler and Toynbee", M. Drout, from an email to me dated 20 March 2009.

4.3.3 *Tolkien was a philologist and also a writer of fiction.* For this reason, and unlike other more "speculative" philologists such as Lachmann or de Saussure, he was not particularly concerned with theoretical concepts, but more so with inspirations for poetical images that the words he studied could give him. He wrote: "History, Philology, Archaeology and Folk-lore were the Fairy-godmothers at the Christening: few [critics of *Beowulf*] thought to invite Poetry" (Drout 2002:80). And Lewis wrote:

> Tolkien thinks that is impossible to invent a language without inventing a mythology, and that the philologist Müller was wrong in calling mythology a disease of language, while it would be truer to say that language was a disease of mythology. I do not understand that. His private mythology clicked with this world at the moment when the participle *atlan* (fallen) which had been produced by sound laws with no anticipation of what it would lead to, when applied to the vanished land of Númenor, turned out to be so obviously connected with our vanished land of Atlantis.
> (Letter to William Kinter, 24 September 1951; Hooper 2004)

4.3.4 *Tolkien was a philologist who lived through two World Wars.* Earlier you said that Tolkien was "very interested in the thought of Boethius; but even *more* interested in adapting that thought to his own circumstances, which were, we should never forget, shaped by two World Wars."[45] You also mentioned his schoolfellow General Slim and Tolkien's slow writing of *The Lord of the Rings* during the Second World War. As you know, I think that that period and the whole tragic episode of the war deeply influenced the composition of the work and that Tolkien intended his book on the "War of the Ring" as his own contribution to the time of war.[46] So he had to *act*, like a soldier, not *speculate*; but life changes, and the time for speculations arrived in later years. At the end of the 1950s, when he was ready to retire, he began to write a lot of explicitly philosophical writings – now collected by his son in *Morgoth's Ring* – on important themes such as the nature of hope, the nature of evil, the relationship between body and soul, and the nature of death.[47]

---

45 See p. 43 above
46 As I tried to demonstrate in Manni 2008.
47 I discussed these "philosophical years", the last fifteen of Tolkien's life, in Manni 2012.

5. *Lewis influenced Tolkien in certain ways.* I suggest that this happened during their twenty years of close friendship. If this is true, it would be useful to know something about Lewis as a philosopher.[48]

5.1 In his letters Lewis makes references to almost all the Classics in the history of philosophy, but he defined himself an Aristotelian.[49]

5.2 Lewis felt that the "ordinary man" had a natural need of philosophy at least *sensu lato*, and wrote: "I also deny that the ordinary man, with his mind full of images and poor in concepts, is really any nearer to the poet than to the philosopher. For the poet uses images as such, because they are images; the ordinary man (that is, all of us from most of our waking hours) uses them *faute de mieux* to attain knowledge, i.e. his end is the same as the philosopher's."[50]

5.3 Lewis neither liked nor respected philosophers who were his contemporaries,[51] probably for two different reasons, both shared with Tolkien: 1) Lewis was not interested in the philosophical schools of his time that were not Christian;[52] 2) he had in general little sympathy with anything that was modern and fashionable.[53]

---

48 It is a pity that in a volume entirely concerned with this very topic the contributors do look for factual connections between Lewis and the various philosophers, but are content with vague thematic analogies. I am referring to Baggett et al. (eds.). 2008. *C.S. Lewis as Philosopher. Truth, Goodness, Beauty.*

49 Throughout his entire adult life Lewis made references to Aristotle. He wrote, in fact: "I fear that Plato thought the concrete flesh and grass bad, and have no doubts he was wrong." And he writes: "not whole Paganism is pantheistic because of the almost miraculous avoidance of the Pantheistic swamp by Plato and (still more) Aristotle." And: "I appear to be a Thomist because I am often (especially on ethics) following Aristotle where Aquinas is also following Aristotle." And last: "many people think I'm being Thomistic where I'm really being Aristotelian" (letters to Corbin Carnell, 13 October and 10 December 1958, Hooper 2007).

50 Letter to Dom Bede Griffiths, 23 May 1936 (Hooper 2004).

51 His letters contain numerous references to (e.g.) Thomas Aquinas, but hardly any to G. Ryle, none to L. Wittgenstein, B. Russell, A.J. Ayer, J. Dewey or the *Wienerkreis*. Writing of the death of J.A. Smith, Lewis says that he was an honest man but an unbeliever, and says nothing about his philosophical ideas. His position is the same with respect to Carritt, Bradley, Joachim, Collingwood, Bosanquet and the other Oxford and Cambridge philosophers, who are hardly ever mentioned in his letters.

52 For example, Lewis made no comment when the analytical philosopher G. Ryle took the chair previously occupied by the idealist R.G. Collingwood at Magdalene College (letter to Martin Moyniahan, 21 May 1944; Hooper 2004).

53 Lewis was aware of the fact: "I am conscious of a partly pathological hostility to what is fashionable. I may therefore be betrayed into statements (or at least, what is perhaps more insidious, a tone) on psychoanalysis which I am not prepared to defend" (letter to Mary Neylan, 26 March 1940; Hooper 2004).

5.4 However, from the beginning of the 1920s he began to turn from professional philosophy and dedicate himself to literature. Although he recognized the "higher" status of the former he considered it too rarefied and solitude-inducing because understood by few.[54]

6. *Some conclusions.*

6.1 You asked earlier: "How would Boethius have coped with Hitler?"[55] – meaning that the question is whether we need to explore the thought of ancient philosophers to become philosophers ourselves, since they did not know some of the things that we do know. In response I would like to quote a saying of the medieval monk Alcuin that you yourself like to quote: *Quid Hinieldus cum Christo? Angusta est domus, utrosque tenere non poterit*,[56] though for the purpose of criticizing it: We *can* keep both Hinieldus and Christus, since, like John of Salisbury, we can say: *Dicebat Bernardus Carnotensis nos esse quasi nanos gigantium humeris insidentes, ut possimus plura eis et remotiora videre, non utique proprii visus acumine, aut eminentia corporis, sed quia in altum subvehimur et extollimur magnitudine gigantea.*[57] I mean by this that although it is true that we do not need direct knowledge of ancient philosophers to philosophise ourselves, nevertheless we need their thought to philosophise *well* (avoiding false paths and blind alleys, shallow and banal truths, and narrow points of view isolated from those of other peoples and cultures).

6.2 Summing up what I said before on Tolkien and the history of philosophy:

- *I am quite sure* he read (at least to some extent) Plato, Aristotle, Augustine, Boethius and Aquinas;

- *I suggest* that he read something of Schlegel, Schopenhauer, Croce, Spengler and perhaps – but I admit it is rather improbable – Vico;[58]

---

54 Letter to his father 14 August 1925 (Hooper 2004).
55 See p. 43 above.
56 "For what has Ingeld to do with Christ? The house is narrow. It cannot contain them both."
57 "Bernard of Chartres used to say that we were like dwarfs seated on the shoulders of giants. If we see more and further than they, it is not due to our own clear eyes or tall bodies, but because we are raised on high and upborne by their gigantic bigness" (John of Salisbury 1955:167).
58 Marek Oziewicz (2008) writes that, to his knowledge, Tolkien had not read Vico because Vico's *New Science* was translated into English only in 1948. But the English translation of the paramount study on Vico, that by Croce, was published in 1913 and executed by R.G. Collingwood, later Tolkien's colleague at Pembroke College.

- *I am sure* that the ideas of Romanticist philosophers such as Schlegel, Herder, Schleiermacher, Fichte, Schelling and Hegel and the ideas of Positivist philosophers such as Comte and Spencer were familiar to Tolkien, indirectly via the great 19th century philologists who knew – sometimes well – their thought;

- *I think* that Tolkien probably had some knowledge of the ideas of contemporary philosophers: Neo-idealists, Logical Positivists, Neo-realists and Existentialists – from Lewis and other scholars of his acquaintance – but that he was not the slightest bit interested in them (just as Lewis and the other Inklings were not).

6.3 I admit to have searched for Tolkien's philosophical "sources" and agree with your comment on Tolkien's "soup" metaphor: "I think source-study can be useful, and that philosophers were no doubt among Tolkien's sources. But Tolkien was right in that it is very difficult to analyse soup into its component parts."[59] I do agree with you that it is very difficult!

Tom Shippey

I have only two things to say here. The first is about the question of influence. C.S. Lewis said that Tolkien was not influenceable, and Franco has pointed out that he clearly was. Perhaps I can reconcile these two statements.

We tend to think of people being influenced positively: they read something, they admire it, they imitate it. But there is another kind of influence, which I will call the influence of provocation, and to this Tolkien was especially liable. The obvious example is indeed Wagner. Wagner was positively influenced by the "Saga of the Volsungs", and re-created it in his operas of *The Nibelung's Ring*. Tolkien, I suspect, thought that Wagner had created a travesty of the original story. So he set himself to correct Wagner's errors – and this is what we now have in Tolkien's "Legend of Sigurd and Gudrún", written in the 1930s but published only in 2009.[60] The same "influence by provocation" is true, in Tolkien's case, of Shakespeare, and of other major poets in the English

---

59 See p. 44 above.
60 See my long review of the work in *Tolkien Studies* 7 (2010):291-324.

tradition. If we had access to Tolkien's rewriting of the Arthurian story, I expect we would find him once again "correcting" Sir Thomas Malory's *Le Morte D'Arthur*.[61]

I call what authors like Tolkien do, "writing into the gap". They see a gap in an established story, or cycle of stories, and they fill the gap. Since we are in Modena, may I point out that this is what Lodovico Ariosto and before him Matteo Boiardo did? Boiardo saw the gap in the Charlemagne legends – they lacked a love interest! – and he wrote into it with his *Orlando Innamorato*.

> Fo gloriosa Bertagna la grande
> Una stagion per l'arme e per l'amore, […]
> Re Carlo in Franza poi tenne gran corte,
> Ma a quella prima non fo sembiante, […]
> Perché tenne ad Amor chiuse le porte.
> (Book 2, canto 18, stanzas 1-2)

Writing into the gap is often a very fruitful exercise.

Did Tolkien see a philosophical gap? Perhaps he did, and one sign of it is that the philosophers I am thinking of include two whom Franco has mentioned only in passing. They are G.E. Moore, who wrote *Principia Ethica* (1903) – note the almost ridiculously ambitious title – and Bertrand Russell, co-author of *Principia Mathematica* (3 volumes, 1910-13). Both men were members of what is now called the Bloomsbury Group, which also included the economist John Maynard Keynes, and the novelists E.M. Forster and Virginia Woolf. This group was the absolute opposite of the Inklings. The "Bloomsberries" were rich, famous, extremely upper-class, intellectually dominant in the between-war period, and they were celebrities. By contrast the Inklings in the 1920s and 1930s were unknown, unsuccessful, out of touch. The Bloomsberries were also atheists, pacifists, theoretical socialists. What had they to tell us about philosophy?

I am not a philosopher, so I don't know. But I read as much as I could of *Principia Ethica*, and found it totally useless. What it seemed to me to propose was what the Bloomsberries in general proposed, which is that the foundation of ethics is personal relations. That is what E.M. Forster always wrote about – his novels

---

61 This has happened in the meantime with the publication of Tolkien's *The Fall of Arthur*.

are novels of sexual and emotional awakening, for members of the privileged but emotionally stunted English upper class. He is famous for having written that if he had to choose between betraying his friends and betraying his country, he hoped he would have the courage to betray his country. This provocative statement was rather spoiled when we found out that far too many members of Forster's Cambridge had in fact been busily betraying their country, with results paid for, with their lives, by people far lower down the social ladder.[62]

There is an old distinction made between private virtue and public virtue. The Bloomsberries focused obsessively on private virtue. This was a luxury which, in the earlier twentieth century, only members of a privileged and sheltered and protected class could afford. The rest of us, in Europe, had to think about much more important things, like being killed in battle, or by bombardment, or in concentration camps. One thing I can say about *The Lord of the Rings* is that it celebrates public virtue. Frodo is indeed a very private person. He would very much like to stay in the Shire (England) and cultivate personal relationships. He does not. He goes into Mordor because it is his duty. To this he sacrifices his emotional development – there is no Rosie Cotton for him, no wife or child – his health and his happiness. E.M. Forster's motto was "Only connect…" Frodo disconnects. The Bloomsberries' lustre has faded now: the world could not afford their self-indulgence. But I think the Inklings, in the 1930s and 1940s, were very aware of them, perhaps enviously, perhaps angrily.

The second thing I have to say is that I agree with Franco in seeing Tolkien as an orphan. Orphans and exiles very much wish to find a home, and if they cannot find one, they invent one. Tolkien decided that his home was Worcestershire, he identified himself with his mother's family, the Suffields, who had lived in Worcestershire for as long as anyone could remember, and he even suggested that his familiarity with the medieval dialects of the West Midlands was somehow inherited, bred in the bone. Professionally, he must have known this could

---

62 The reference here is to Guy Burgess (1911-1963) and Kim Philby (1912-1988), two members of the "Cambridge Five", a group of English spies working during 1940s and 1950s for the USSR. Shippey noted that in the book by Martin Green, *Children of the Sun* (New York: Basic Books Publisher, 1976, 369-70), Burgess and Philby prove to have a close connection with the Bloomsberries, and especially with Forster.

not be true: we are quite sure that language is not transmitted genetically. But Tolkien wanted to believe it.

Franco has suggested an opposition between Grimm's attempts to recover the past, and the belief in "re-enactment" which he ascribes to Hegel, Croce, Collingwood. I think that Tolkien perhaps mediated between these two views. Briefly, like Grimm, Tolkien was all his life fascinated by what I have called "survivor genres": those aspects of the modern world which show an unbroken continuity with the ancient past, a continuity which has been forgotten and which is usually, and especially by the intellectual and social upper classes like the Bloomsberries, ignored or despised. The obvious example is fairy-tales – which of course the Grimms collected so assiduously. But there are also nursery-rhymes, and riddles – Tolkien wrote and published examples of both – and proverbial sayings, which are so important to the hobbits, and (something of great importance to Tolkien) the names of places and of people. He thought his Aunt Jane Neave bore the name of a forgotten hero, the Danish hero Hnaef, remembered in Anglo-Saxon poetry. He thought the heroic tradition of pre-Norman England had not gone away, though no-one was any longer aware of it. It was there like courage in the heart of Bilbo Baggins, waiting to be re-awakened: as Gandalf says, "The old that is strong does not wither […] From the ashes a fire shall be woken" (*LotR* FR.I.x). So, on the one hand there is the Grimmian urge to rediscover the lost world, to "write into the gap", as I put it. But on the other there is the insistence that this lost world has not really gone away, that it has never been quite forgotten, that it is possible to re-enact it – maybe, even, that it is impossible *not* to re-enact it, because it is bred in the bone and rooted in the homeland.

What I do not know is whether this second feeling is true or not. Is it a recognition of a real truth? Or is it an illusion, created above all by the orphan's wish to find a father and have a home?

5. Providence in *The Lord of the Rings*

Franco Manni

Until now we have dealt with the relationships between philologists, in particular the philologist Tolkien, and philosophers and the history of philosophy. A difficult but productive topic for discussion, as we have seen, and also one given very little treatment in criticism of Tolkien. Books and articles on Tolkien's "philosophy" tend to concentrate on themes without attempting to identify specific historical relationships with individual philosophers or philosophical schools. Now, Tom, let's finish with a discussion of the philosophical *theme* present in Tolkien's fiction.

There are numerous possibilities (such as power, death and immortality, the philosophy of history etc.), but I ask you to discuss just one: Providence. When I interviewed you years ago,[63] you said that in the 19th century some of the great figures of English literature wrote about Providence – for example George Eliot and Charles Dickens – whereas you do not know of any 20th-century novels that deal with it, apart from those of Tolkien. In *Roots and Branches* you wrote, in fact, that providence is the "philosophical heart" of *The Lord of the Rings* (Shippey 2007:383).

Tom Shippey

My subject is Providence, as seen especially in *The Lord of the Rings*, and, since our topic is "Tolkien and Philosophy", perhaps I may begin by quoting the words of Philosophy herself. Boethius's famous work, *De Consolatione Philosophiae*, consists of a dialogue between Boethius and Lady Philosophy. Boethius, a Roman senator, had been condemned to death and was indeed executed by Theodoric, the Gothic king of Italy. In prison, and awaiting execution, he imagines himself complaining to Philosophy, and being consoled by what she has to say.

His main complaint is about injustice, the injustice which has led to his own condemnation, but which leaves wicked men free and apparently happy. Philosophy

---

[63] See Manni and Shippey 2005.

persuades him that this is not so, that the wicked are never happy and the virtuous are always fortunate. Boethius continues to express doubt. In Book 4, prose 5 he asks how the operation of Providence differs from that of chance, or fate, and confesses that he would be less troubled if he did believe that the world was run by Chance. What reason can be found, he asks, for so unjust a state of disorder?

> *Minus etenim mirarer si misceri omnia fortuitis casibus crederem. Nunc stuporem meum deus rector exaggerat. Qui cum saepe bonis iucunda, malis aspera contraque bonis dura tribuat, malis optata concedat, nisi causa deprehenditur, quid est quod a fortuitis casibus differre uideatur?*
>
> For assuredly I should wonder less if I could believe that all things are the confused result of chance. But now my belief in God's governance adds amazement to amazement. For, seeing that He sometimes assigns fair fortune to the good and harsh fortune to the bad, and then again deals harshly with the good, and grants to the bad their hearts' desire, how does this differ from chance, unless some reason is discovered for it all?[64]

Philosophy replies, with a smile (prose 6), that this is the hardest question to deal with, for it involves many issues.

> *Ad rem me, inquit, omnium quaesitu maximam uocas, cui uix exhausti quicquam satis sit. Talis namque materia est ut una dubitatione succisa innumerabiles aliae uelut hydrae capita succrescant; necullus fuerit modus nisi quis eas uiuacissimo mentis igne coherceat. In hac enim de prouidentiae simplicitate, de fati serie, de repentinis casibus, de cognitione ac praedestinatione diuina, de arbitrii libertate quaeri solet, quae quanti oneris sit ipse perpendis.*
>
> You call me, she said, to the greatest of all subjects of inquiry, a task for which the most exhaustive treatment barely suffices. Such is its nature that, as fast as one doubt is cut away, innumerable others spring up like Hydra's heads, nor could we set any limit to their renewal did we not apply the mind's living fire to suppress them. For there come within its scope the questions of the essential simplicity of providence, of the order of fate, of unforeseen chance, of the Divine knowledge and predestination, and of the freedom of the will. How heavy is the weight of all this you can judge for yourself.

Like the heads of the Hydra, then, the questions of Providence and Fate, of divine foreknowledge and free will, are all intertwined.

---

64 The Latin text here is from G. Weinberger's 1935 edition for the *Corpus Scriptorum Ecclesiasticorum Latinorum*, vol. 67, while the English translation is that of W.V. Cooper for the *Temple Classics* edition of 1902. Both are available on www9.georgetown.edu/faculty/jod/boethius/jkok/list_t.htm

So, Philosophy tells us that Providence is the hardest question to answer, and I believe her. However, I do not believe (and indeed I have great difficulty in understanding) her answer and explanation, especially the part where she concludes that "All fortune is good fortune" – even an unjust death sentence. Like everyone else, I give Boethius great credit for courage in writing this work, while waiting for a cruel execution, but I myself do not find the work satisfying or convincing. I've also suggested that Tolkien likewise did not find it possible to agree entirely with Boethius, and I went so far as to argue[65] that there are two philosophical principles in Tolkien, and especially in *The Lord of the Rings*, and they are those represented by the orthodox Catholic Boethius and by the heretic Manichaeus (though both these represent views held by many others: I use the names just as convenient labels for a position).

The Boethian view is an orthodox Christian one, and contains several beliefs which Tolkien certainly shared and expressed in *The Lord of the Rings*, such as these:

1. Nothing is evil in the beginning, nothing has been created evil by the Creator. Gandalf says very plainly, "nothing is evil in the beginning. Even Sauron was not so" (*LotR* FR.II.ii).

2. Evil is in any case an absence, not a presence: the point is made graphically at the gate of Minas Tirith when the Chief Ringwraith sweeps back his hood, and there is nothing underneath (*LotR* RK.V.iv).

3. Evil, then, cannot create: Frodo says of the orcs, "The Shadow that bred them can only mock, it cannot make" (*LotR* RK.VI.i).

Tolkien had difficulty, however, in reconciling some of these statements with his story, most especially over the orcs. If evil cannot create, where did they come from? Were they creatures initially good, or capable of good, who had been corrupted? Could this corruption be inherited? Had they free will? I do not think Tolkien ever solved this problem to his own satisfaction.[66]

What I have suggested, in fact, is that the world of *The Lord of the Rings* appears in some ways to be a Manichaean one, in which forces of evil fight forces of

---

65 Shippey (2005: ch. 5, especially 159-66).
66 As one can see from his notes gathered together in *Morgoth* 408-24.

good, and they exist on a basis of apparent equality. In suggesting this, I knew that Tolkien would very much *not* have liked the suggestion, for Manichaeus was a heretic, and Tolkien was an orthodox Catholic, and would have hated the idea that he was presenting a heretical view. Nevertheless, there do seem to be two views of evil present in his work. In the orthodox or Boethian one, evil is a process of corruption, to which we are all subject. So, the Ring works on people by appealing to something inside themselves. In the unorthodox or Manichaean view, evil is a force from outside us, which can bend us to its will regardless of our resistance. So, the Ring has a will of its own, to betray Isildur, to desert Gollum, to make Frodo return it to its master.

Note that this unorthodox view is probably the one that most of us believe. It is the view of common experience. I know that I have impulses to evil. However, most of the time I experience evil as something which is forced upon me and which I can do little or nothing about. In Tolkien's lifetime this view was even more obvious: those killed in the concentration camps, the bombing raids, the great military campaigns, were just victims of forces from outside. I thought that the tension between the orthodox and unorthodox views of evil was one of the factors which made *The Lord of the Rings* such a powerful work, and so expressive of the problems of the twentieth century, in which it became harder and harder to believe Boethius's statement, and Philosophy's, that "all fortune is good fortune."

Now, I have been told since that I misunderstood Boethius and Manichaeus and Lady Philosophy too, and this is very likely, since (as I keep on saying) I am not a philosopher. My friend John Houghton has explained[67] that Tolkien's view was in fact strictly orthodox, in line with Church doctrine, and deriving ultimately from St Augustine; and I am very ready to believe him: for Dr Houghton is a learned man, and furthermore a priest in Anglican orders, so if there is any dispute about theology, his view is much more likely to be correct than mine is. However, since I am not a philosopher, when Dr Houghton tells me that Tolkien's view is "consistently paradoxical rather than ambiguous or contradictory" (151), I am inclined to say: "Oh. I believe you. What is the difference, exactly?" And in any case, how does this help me to understand

---

67 In Houghton and Keesee 2005.

evil? How does it help me to see the workings of a benevolent Providence in what appears to be mere Chance? How does it help me to reconcile divine foreknowledge with my own feeling that I have free will to do good or bad? These are difficult questions for someone who is not a philosopher. Fortunately, I think I have come to understand them much better from Tolkien than I ever did from Boethius.

In *The Lord of the Rings*, Tolkien never uses the word "providence" – I can say this thanks to Franco, who provided me with a machine-searchable text of the work. On the other hand, he uses the word "fate" many times, and "chance" many times as well. So, on the face of it, Tolkien was much more conscious of fate and chance than of providence. But that is not the case. I can begin by noting that there are a few places where Tolkien expresses doubt, or allows his characters to express doubt, about the very existence of chance. Gandalf, for instance, talking to Frodo and Gimli after the War of the Ring is over, says we might call the death of King Dáin of the dwarves sad: "Yet things might have gone far otherwise and far worse […] But that has been averted – because I met Thorin Oakenshield one evening on the edge of spring in Bree. A chance-meeting, *as we say in Middle-earth*" (*LotR* App.A.III; emphasis added). The implication of the words I have emphasised is that *outside* Middle-earth, in the Undying Lands, the meeting would not have been seen as chance at all. And this is suggested several times elsewhere. Tom Bombadil, for instance, says of his rescue of the hobbits from the Willow-man, "just chance brought me then, *if chance you call it*" (*LotR* FR.I.vii). The implication again is that chance is just a word, and a misleading one.

Having remembered those two familiar qualifications, I then took Franco's text of *The Lord of the Rings* and asked it to find all cases of the words "chance or": there were three of them. Then I tried "or chance", and there was another. Then I tried "or fate", and there were two more, as well as one similar case which I happened to remember. So I found in total some seven more cases where chance or fate were proposed as explanations for events – but queried, like Gandalf's and Bombadil's doubts as to whether their meetings were really "by chance". Three of these seem to me to be especially significant for Tolkien's philosophy of providence.

The first comes when Merry and Pippin are being carried off by the Sauron-orc Grishnákh from the Saruman-orcs, just as the Riders of Rohan attack. Grishnákh draws a knife to kill them so they cannot be rescued, but an arrow from one of the Riders hits him. It was "aimed with skill, or guided by fate" (*LotR* TT.III.iii). Which? We can't tell. But if it wasn't "aimed with skill", if it was just a random shot, then why say it was "guided"? "Guided" implies a Guide, and a deliberate intention. Maybe other things which seem to be random are also intended, by some force we do not know.

That is what Gildor Inglorion the elf thinks. He meets Frodo as Frodo and his friends are leaving the Shire, and scares off the Black Riders. He is reluctant to give Frodo any advice, because, he says:

> The Elves have their own labours and their own sorrows, and they are little concerned with the ways of hobbits, or of any other creatures upon earth. Our paths cross theirs seldom, by chance or purpose. In this meeting there may be more than chance; but the purpose is not clear to me, and I fear to say too much. (LotR FR.I.iii)

This implies again that like Gandalf and Thorin, Frodo and Gildor have not had a "chance-meeting". It was purposed, but not by them. Are they then being "guided" by unknown forces, and if they are, are we? Are we in fact puppets of some unknown Controller? As Lady Philosophy said, the issue of chance is bound up with the issue of Providence, and the issue of Providence with the issue of free will.

Gandalf has a comment to make on this, in which the idea of fate is very clearly qualified, this time by free will. When Gandalf sees Frodo recovering in Rivendell from the knife-wound of the Black Rider, he says he was lucky to survive: "fortune or fate have helped you, not to mention courage. For your heart was not touched, and only your shoulder was pierced; and that was because you resisted to the last" (*LotR* FR.II.i). Maybe fate helped Frodo. But it might *not* have done if he had not helped fate – by exercising his free will in resisting.

These phrases do not tell us very much or very clearly,[68] but they do suggest there are forces at work in *The Lord of the Rings*, and one of those forces, I suggest, is the one we perceive as chance, but which is in fact the way that Providence works – Providence, the never-mentioned force. Is it right to detect in Tolkien's work something which he never once mentions? I suggest that this is implicit in the whole structure of volumes 2 and 3 of *The Lord of the Rings*. It is a very complex structure, one might even say an unnecessarily complex structure – unless it is there to draw our attention to something.

Let me just remind you first, philosophically, of what Philosophy eventually says about Providence to Boethius. She explains to him that we humans are basically not equipped to understand the nature of Providence, because we perceive things in time, one after another, and we perceive them also as they affect only ourselves: we have only limited knowledge of what happens outside our own view. We don't know where things come from, whether they are arrows, or meetings, or other people. But the Divine Mind is not like that. It sees everything that happens, has happened, will happen, all at once. It sees connections where we see only disconnected events. It can guide events to create results we cannot foresee. It can take account of our own reactions to those events to set up further events. Boethius uses an image of a turning wheel. At the very centre, nothing moves. At the extremes, there is the continual change of Fortune's Wheel. King Alfred, translating Boethius with many changes into Anglo-Saxon, makes this clearer by saying the wheel is a cartwheel, which rests on an axle, has a hub, and spokes, and rim-pieces. We are all on the wheel, but the worldly are furthest away from the unmoving axle – I think Anglo-Saxon axles did not rotate, the wheel rotated round the axle – and the further away from the axle you are, the more you feel under the power of chance, or fate, or fortune. But these are just words – and for philological reasons I would add another word to the list, which is "luck" – and they are all words for "the way that human beings perceive the operations of Providence."

---

68 My other four examples are: *LotR* TT.III.viii ("by design or chance", the double meaning of Orthanc); *LotR* TT.IV.iv ("his life is charmed, or fate spares him", Faramir); *LotR* App.A.I ("by chance or by foresight", the counsel of the Lossoth or Snowmen); *LotR* App.A.II ("by chance or design", the Orcs' attack on Gondor defeated by Eorl the Young).

The way Tolkien presents this, in *The Lord of the Rings*, is by showing people who are disconnected from each other, but who are always affected by the actions of others, of which they know nothing. We see at once, as we read *The Lord of the Rings*, the limited perception of the characters, and some hint of the overall connected perception of Providence. It is easy to see what I mean about the characters being disconnected. At the end of *The Fellowship of the Ring* the Fellowship is all together (apart from Gandalf). At the start of *The Two Towers* they are separated. Sam and Frodo have gone off in one direction. Merry and Pippin have been taken in another. Aragorn, Legolas and Gimli follow them. They are rejoined in Fangorn Forest by Gandalf, and go to Meduseld with him. But then Gandalf leaves them again, riding off to find Merry and Pippin – to their great surprise, for they believe he is dead. Then he goes back to Aragorn and his companions. The six members of the Fellowship only meet at Isengard, but they do not stay together for long, for Pippin goes off with Gandalf to Minas Tirith, Merry remains with the Riders of Rohan, and Aragorn, Legolas and Gimli take the Path of the Dead. They meet again on the Field of Cormallen. Meanwhile, and all the time, Sam and Frodo, and now Gollum, are struggling towards Mordor.

This extremely complex form of narration (which I have had to simplify) has several effects. Each group of characters does not know what the others are doing. Nevertheless, what they do is continually affected by actions they do not know about. Aragorn, Legolas and Gimli set off to save Merry and Pippin. In fact, they are saved by Merry and Pippin, who set the Ents in motion. Then Pippin in Minas Tirith is saved by Merry and the arrival of the Riders. Merry, at the Battle of the Pelennor Fields, is saved by the arrival of Aragorn. All of them, in the end, are saved by Sam and Frodo. But Sam and Frodo could never have completed their mission if it had not been for the actions of Pippin, who retrieved the *palantír* from Saruman, and Aragorn, who showed himself in the *palantír* to Sauron, deliberately, to draw Sauron's attention to him. The point is made very neatly in the third Jackson movie, when Sam and Frodo, wondering how they can cross the plain of Gorgoroth, see the orcs' camp-fires going out and the orcs leaving. "That's a stroke of luck", says Sam. *But he is wrong.* It is not luck. It is a result of Aragorn's deliberate design, of which Sam knows nothing. *Or maybe it is luck.* What we call "luck" is often the result of other people's actions. And the totality of other people's actions forms a design which is set by Providence. But the bits we see of it, in our partial vision, we call "luck", or "chance", or in Anglo-Saxon, *wyrd*. King Alfred (if he it was) put the case simply: "Once something's happened, then we call it *wyrd* [that is, 'fate' or 'luck']; before that [when it was still only in the Divine Mind] it was God's forethought and his Providence."[69]

One of the results of Tolkien's method of narration is that, on the one hand, the reader encounters repeated surprises, where he or she knows less than the characters: no-one expects to come upon Merry and Pippin smoking quietly in the ruins of Isengard, because we last saw them looking down into the Wizard's Vale, with Isengard still unharmed. No-one expects Aragorn to appear from the Great River in the Corsairs' ships, because we last saw him coming out of the Path of the Dead. No-one expects Gandalf to re-appear from Moria. When he does re-appear, for all Aragorn and his companions know, this White Wizard is Saruman.

Conversely, there are moments of irony, where the reader knows more than the characters do. Aragorn's attempt to track the hobbit's escape from the orcs baffles him. But not us: we know what happened. The death of Théoden may seem like "bad luck" to the characters, but not to us. We know what caused it: it was Denethor. His attempted suicide and murder of Faramir, reported by Pippin, are what drew Gandalf from the battlefield. "Where is Gandalf?" thinks Merry. "Could he not have saved the king and Éowyn?" (*LotR* RK.V.vi). But when Pippin asks Gandalf, "Can't you save Faramir?" Gandalf answers, "Maybe I can, but if I do, others will die." (*LotR* RK.V.vii). We know who those others are. At the time of speaking, Gandalf does not. But we know his words are true.

The Lord of the Rings then does two things. It shows us actions as they are perceived by the characters, when they appear to be the result of chance. But it also shows us that they are the result of chains of decision, which form a pattern we may well call Providential. There is no doubt about the free will of the characters, who must make their own decisions with no idea whether they are

---

69 Godden and Irvine (eds.). 2009. *The Old English Boethius*. Vol. 1, 262, my translation.

correct or not: Aragorn has to do this continually, and at one point he seems to lose heart, saying to Legolas "You give the choice to an ill chooser [...] Since we passed through the Argonath my choices have gone amiss" (*LotR* TT.III.ii). Gandalf, however, points out that things have not gone amiss, but unexpectedly well, for "between them our enemies have contrived only to bring Merry and Pippin with marvellous speed, and in the nick of time, to Fangorn, where otherwise they would never have come at all!" (*LotR* TT.III.v).

There are many such cross-references, not all of them immediately clear. We might have thought it was "luck" which saved Frodo from the Eye of Sauron on Amon Hen (*LotR* FR.II.x). It wasn't, it was Gandalf. But we only find that out sixty pages later (*LotR* TT.III.v) – and inattentive readers may never realise at all. The most important cross-reference, in my opinion – but there are those who disagree,[70] and many more who have never noticed the point – comes from the *palantíri*. These continually deceive their users. Pippin looks in the Orthanc stone, and Sauron assumes that this hobbit is the Ring-Bearer, and that Saruman must have both stone and Ring. Then Aragorn looks in the Orthanc stone, and Sauron assumes that since he has the stone, Aragorn now must have the Ring, making his attack on Minas Tirith too early as a result. But then Denethor looks in the Minas Tirith stone, and sees what Sauron (or his own fear?) leads him to see, which is Frodo, as a prisoner. Denethor assumes that Sauron has the Ring, and decides to commit suicide as a result. First Sauron, then Denethor, are deceived. What they are trying to do is to guess what will happen next, and to shape their actions accordingly. That is a terrible mistake, as Galadriel says to Sam after he has looked in her Mirror. "Some [things] never come to be, unless those that behold the visions turn aside from their path to prevent them" (*LotR* FR.II.vii).

Make your own decisions. Do not try to guess better than Providence. Providence is the result of all decisions. It weaves them together in its own Providential

---

70 For my view, see Shippey (2000: 172-73). For a counter-argument, see Jessica Yates 2009. I do not entirely follow Yates's argument, but there should be no doubt that Denethor commits suicide because he is sure Sauron now has the Ring, as confirmed by his words "The fool's hope has failed. The Enemy has found it" (*LotR* RK.V.iv). The phrase "fool's hope" has been used twice earlier in the same chapter to refer to Gandalf's plan of sending the Ring to Mordor. Thanks to Franco's invaluable machine-searchable text, we know the phrase is never used to mean anything else. The "it" the Enemy has found can only be the Ring.

pattern. No human can know how that will work, for "[e]ven the wise cannot see all ends" (*LotR* TT.IV.i).

I find this really a clear statement, much clearer in fact than what Philosophy says to Boethius, but essentially the same. It is put, however, in un-philosophical language, as a story, not as an argument, as a set of examples, not a thesis. Being a philologist and not a philosopher, I find examples much easier to understand than a general principle, though I can draw a general principle from the examples.

I'd like to close by saying that Tolkien was not the only English author to come to this conclusion. One of the classic novelists of the 19th century was George Eliot, the pen-name of a female author who by the way was an admirer of Grimm. Her short novel *Silas Marner* (1861) tells the story of a string of disasters: a miser robbed of his gold, a little girl lost, a father disappeared, a thief whose crime does not come to light. It is also remarkable – philologists like this – in being one of the very few English novels of any period in which *no-one at all* speaks standard English: they all speak one form or another of provincial dialect. At the end, events are summed up not by an educated speaker, but by Dolly Varden, a poor countrywoman who speaks only her own dialect. She has a long speech, which is really about Providence – she says, we see only parts of events, and they may appear to us as disasters. But if we saw them whole, maybe they would not. All we can do, she says, is "to trusten [i.e. to trust]". Yet one more strange thing about her speech is that it is clearly a paraphrase of *De Consolatione Philosophiae* Book IV prose 6 – but although her novel has been many times studied and edited and annotated, I do not think my colleagues in the literary field of English Studies have ever noticed. Why would they? Boethius wrote in Latin. He is not part of the English syllabus. We do not do Philosophy in English departments.

All this, alas, is part of what I said earlier: the increasing compartmentalisation of studies in the modern university. But without philosophy we cannot always understand fiction. And, alas, without fiction, I at any rate cannot well understand philosophy. Tolkien, then, along with his friend Lewis, has been one of the great communicators of philosophy to the modern world, which is in danger of forgetting it.

About the Authors

FRANCO MANNI obtained two degrees in Philosophy and Theology respectively. Since 1999 he has been editing a Tolkienian journal, *Endòre*, and several Tolkien-related books: *Introduzione a Tolkien, Tolkien e la Terra di Mezzo, Mitopoiesi, Lettera a un amico della Terra di Mezzo*, and the Italian translation of Shippey's *J.R.R. Tolkien: Author of the Century*. He also published two papers in English, one in the Proceedings of the 2005 Birmingham Tolkien Conference, and one in *Mallorn*.

TOM SHIPPEY has written widely on Old English, Old Norse, and other medieval topics, but is best known for his three books on Tolkien, *The Road to Middle-earth* (4th ed., 2004), *J.R.R. Tolkien: Author of the Century* (2000), and *Roots and Branches: Selected Papers on Tolkien* (2007). He is currently a regular reviewer of fantasy and science fiction for *The Wall Street Journal*.

Bibliography

ARDUINI, Roberto and Claudio TESTI (eds.). 2012. *The Broken Scythe. Death and Immortality in the Works of J.R.R. Tolkien*. Jena and Zurich: Walking Tree Publishers.

BAGGETT, D., G. HABERMAS and J. WALLS (eds.). 2008. *C.S. Lewis as Philosopher. Truth, Goodness, Beauty*. Madison: Inter Varsity Press Academic.

BIRZER, B.J. 2007. "Aquinas", in Drout 2007b, 21-22.

BRADLEY, Sid A.J. 2008. *N.F.S. Grundtvig: a Life Recalled. An Anthology of Biographical Source-Texts*. Aarhus: Aarhus University Press.

BURNS, Marjorie. 2007. "Tracking the Elusive Hobbit (In Its Pre-Shire den)." *Tolkien Studies* 4:200-11.

CALDECOTT, Stratford and Thomas HONEGGER (eds.). 2008. *Tolkien's The Lord of the Rings. Sources and Inspirations*. Zurich and Jena: Walking Tree Publishers.

CARPENTER, Humphrey. 1978. *The Inklings. C.S. Lewis, J.R.R. Tolkien, Charles Williams and Their Friends*. London: George Allen & Unwin.

2000. *J.R.R. Tolkien: A Biography*. Boston: Houghton Mifflin.

CARRITT, Edgar F. 1914. *The Theory of Beauty*. New York: The MacMillan Company.

COLLINGWOOD, Robin G. 1992. *The Idea of History*. First Published 1946. Oxford: Oxford University Press.

2005. *The Philosophy of Enchantment: Studies in Folktale, Cultural Criticism, and Anthropology*. Ed. David Boucher, Wendy Jems and Philip Smallwood. Oxford: Clarendon Press.

and John N.L. MYRES. 1936. *Roman Britain and the English Settlements*. Oxford: Oxford University Press.

CROCE, Benedetto. 1913. *The Philosophy of G.B. Vico*. London: Howard Latimer Ltd.

2001. *Teoria e storia della storiografia*. Milano: Adelphi.

DROUT, Michael. 2002. *Beowulf and the Critics*. Tempe AZ: Arizona Medieval and Renaissance Texts and Studies.

2007a. "J.R.R. Tolkien's Medieval Scholarship and its Significance." *Tolkien Studies* 4:113-76.

(ed.). 2007b. *J.R.R. Tolkien Encyclopedia: Scholarship and Critical Assessment*. London: Routledge.

FIESOLI, Giovanni. 2000. *La genesi del lachmannismo*. Firenze: SISMEL Edizioni dal Galluzzo.

FLIEGER, Verlyn and Douglas A. ANDERSON (eds.). 2008. *Tolkien On Fairy Stories*. London: HarperCollins.

GODDEN, Malcolm and Susan IRVINE (eds.). 2009. *The Old English Boethius*. 2 vols. Oxford: Oxford University Press.

GRIMM, Jacob. 1864-1884. *Kleiner Schriften*. Berlin: Dümmler.

GUMBRECHT, Hans U. 2003. *The Powers of Philology. Dynamics of Textual Scholarship*. Urbana, IL: University of Illinois Press.

HAMMOND, Wayne G. and Christina SCULL. 2006a. *The J.R.R. Tolkien Companion and Guide: Chronology*. London: HarperCollins.

2006b. "Addenda and Corrigenda to *The J.R.R. Tolkien Companion and Guide* [2006], Vol. 1: Chronology." http://mysite.verizon.net/wghammon/addenda/chronology.html

HOOKER, Mark. 2011. "Reading John Buchan in Search of Tolkien." In Jason FISHER (ed.). 2011. *Tolkien and the Study of His Sources*. Jefferson, NC: McFarland, 162-192.

HOOPER, Walter (ed.). 2004. *The Collected Letters of C.S. Lewis*. Vols. 1 & 2. New York: HarperCollins.

(ed.). 2007 *The Collected Letters of C.S. Lewis*. Vol. 3. New York: HarperCollins.

HOUGHTON, John and Neal K. KEESEE. 2005. "Tolkien, King Alfred and Boethius." *Tolkien Studies* 2:131-159.

HUTTON, Ronald. 2003. *Witches, Druids and King Arthur*. London and New York: Hambledon.

INGLIS, Fred. 2009. *History Man. The Life of R.G. Collingwood*. Princeton, NJ: Princeton University Press.

JOHN OF SALISBURY. 1955. *Metologicon*. Book III. Berkley and Los Angeles: University of California Press.

LEHMANN, Winfred P. 2003. *Historical Linguistics: An Introduction*. New York: Routledge.

LEWIS, Alex. 2009. "The Ogre in the Dungeon." *Mallorn* 47:15-18.

LEWIS, Clive Staples. 1945. *That Hideous Strength*. London: Bodley Head.

MACLACHLAN, Christopher. 2012. *Tolkien and Wagner: The Ring and Der Ring*. Zurich and Jena: Walking Tree Publishers.

Manni, Franco and Tom Shippey. 2005. "Tolkien autore del XX secolo." In Franco Manni (ed.). 2005. *Mitopoiesi. Fantasia e storia in Tolkien*. Brescia: Grafo edizioni, 175-184.

— (ed.). 2005. *Mitopoiesi. Fantasia e storia in Tolkien*. Brescia: Grafo edizioni.

— 2008. "The Complexity of Tolkien's Attitude Towards the Second World War." In Sarah Wells (ed.). 2008. *The Ring Goes Ever On, Proceedings of the Tolkien 2005 Conference, 50 Years of the Lord of the Rings*. Coventry: The Tolkien Society, 33-51.

— 2012. "An Eulogy of Finitude: Anthropology, Eschatology and Philosophy of History in Tolkien." In Roberto Arduini and Claudio Testi (eds.). 2012. *The Broken Scythe. Death and Immortality in the Works of J.R.R. Tolkien*. Zurich and Jena: Walking Tree Publishers, 5-38.

Marini, Giuliano. 1974. "Jacob Grimm e Vico." *Bollettino di Studi Vichiani*.

Meli, Marcello. 1992. "Jacob Grimm e le origini del linguaggio." In *Jacob Grimm. La parola e la storia*. Milano: Franco Angeli.

Myres, John N.L. 1986. *The English Settlements*. Oxford: Oxford University Press.

Nencioni, Giovanni. 1989. *Idealismo e realismo nella scienza del linguaggio*. Pisa: Scuola Normale Superiore.

Noad, Charles E. 2010. "R.G. Collingwood – Another Tolkien Reference." *Amon Hen* 226:11-12.

Nörr, Dieter. 1994. *Savignys philosophische Lehrjahre*. Frankfurt: Klostermann.

Olender, Maurice. 2008. *The Languages of Paradise. Race, Religion and Philology in the Nineteenth Century*. Cambridge, MA: Harvard University Press.

Oziewicz, Marek. 2008. "From Vico to Tolkien: The Affirmation of Myth Against the Tyranny of Reason." In Stratford Caldecott and Thomas Honegger (eds.). 2008. *Tolkien's The Lord of the Rings. Sources and Inspirations*. Zurich and Jena: Walking Tree Publishers, 113-136.

Reynolds, Patricia and Glen H. Goodknight (eds.). 1995. *Proceedings of the J.R.R. Tolkien Centenary Conference*. Milton Keynes and Altadena: The Tolkien Society & The Mythopoeic Press.

Rückert, Joachim. 1984. *Idealismus, Jurisprudenz und Politik bei Friedrich Carl von Savigny*. Ebelsbach: Gremer.

Seeman, Chris. 1995. "Tolkien's Revision of the Romantic Tradition." In Patricia Reynolds and Glen H. Goodknight (eds.). 1995. *Proceedings of the J.R.R. Tolkien Centenary Conference*. Milton Keynes and Altadena: The Tolkien Society & The Mythopoeic Press, 73-83.

SHIPPEY, Tom. 2000. *J.R.R. Tolkien: Author of the Century*. London: HarperCollins.

2005. *The Road to Middle-earth*. London: HarperCollins.

2007. *Roots and Branches*. Zurich and Berne: Walking Tree Publishers.

TIMPANARO, Sebastiano. 1963. *La genesi del metodo del Lachmann*. Firenze: Le Monnier.

TOEWS, John E. 2004. *Becoming Historical. Cultural Reformation and Public Memory in Early Nineteenth Century Berlin*. Cambridge: Cambridge University Press.

VINK, Renée. 2012. *Wagner and Tolkien: Mythmakers*. Zurich and Jena: Walking Tree Publishers.

VON WILAMOWITZ, Ulrich. 1967. *Storia della filologia classica*. Torino: Einaudi.

WARD, Michael. 2008. *Planet Narnia: The Seven Heavens in the Imagination of C.S. Lewis*. Oxford: Oxford University Press.

WAWN, Andrew. 2000. *The Vikings and the Victorians: Inventing the Old North in Nineteenth century Britain*. Cambridge: D.S. Brewer.

WELLS, Sarah (ed.). 2008. *The Ring Goes Ever On, Proceedings of the Tolkien 2005 Conference, 50 Years of the Lord of the Rings*. Coventry: The Tolkien Society.

YATES, Jessica. 2009. "The Curious Case of Denethor and the *Palantír*." *Mallorn* 47:18-25.

Works by J.R.R. Tolkien

The Fall of Arthur, ed. Christopher Tolkien. London: HarperCollins, 2013.

Letters: *The Letters of J.R.R. Tolkien*, ed. Humphrey Carpenter, with the assistance of Christopher Tolkien. London: George Allen & Unwin, 1981.

LotR: The Lord of the Rings, 50th anniversary edition. Boston: Houghton Mifflin, 2004.

LTP: La trasmissione del pensiero e la numerazione degli Elfi. Milano: Marietti 1820, 2008.

MC: The Monsters and the Critics and Other Essays, ed. Christopher Tolkien. London: George Allen & Unwin 1983. London: HarperCollins, 1997.

Morgoth: Morgoth's Ring (HoMe 10), ed. Christopher Tolkien. London: George Allen & Unwin 1993.

Lost Tales I: *The Book of Lost Tales I* (HoMe 1), ed. Christopher Tolkien. London: George Allen & Unwin 1983.

The Old English Exodus: Text, Translation and Commentary, ed. Joan Turville-Petre, Oxford: Clarendon Press, 1981.

Sauron: *Sauron Defeated* (HoMe 9), ed. Christopher Tolkien. London: George Allen & Unwin 1992.

SG: *The Legend of Sigurd and Gudrun*, ed Christopher Tolkien. London: HarperCollins, 2009.

Verlyn Flieger

Tolkien and the Philosophy of Language

A brief statement in Manuscript A, the 1939 first draft of Tolkien's essay "On Fairy-stories" declares unequivocally that, "Mythology is language and language is mythology" (*TOFS* 181). If I ever put a bumper sticker on my car, it's going to say that. No modifiers, no explanations, just seven words that convey Tolkien's most fundamental belief about words and what they do. Mythology does not *use* language; it *is* language – in shape and sound and meaning. Language does not *express* mythology; it *is* mythology – on the hoof, in action, alive and moving. In this sense, the whole text of "On Fairy-stories" is an extended gloss on that statement. The next sentence in the draft, "The mind, the tongue, and the tale, are coeval" (*TOFS* 181), adds what is implicit in the bumper-sticker, the perceiving human consciousness that is the necessary link between mythology and language. The 1934 B draft which became the published essay dropped the bumper sticker dictum but kept the mind, the tongue and the tale (*TOFS* 221), and addressed the implicit question: "To ask what is the origin of stories, is to ask what is the origin of the mind, and of language" (*TOFS* 218).

Taking "language" to mean words arranged in a meaningful pattern and "mythology" to mean the world-view of a culture carried by its stories of gods and heroes, we can read all three statements as variations on the theme that language, stories, and story-tellers together make up an interlocking, interdependent system. There is no story without a teller, no teller without a language, no language without something to talk about. Without a world to report, and without the people who live in that world to do the reporting, language has no use. Tolkien's description in the same essay of Faërie as containing "the seas, the sun, the moon, the sky; and the earth and all things that are in it: tree and bird, water and stone, wine and bread, and ourselves, mortal men" (*TOFS* 32) illustrates the process. The listed items are the phenomena of a world, brought into being by the words that name them.

Though it is one of the bases of his creative method, the idea is not original to Tolkien. It comes from a particular school of linguistic thought that developed out of 19th century German Romanticism, found a home in comparative philology and mythology, and was expressed in the ideas of Owen Barfield, a philosopher of language and part of that circle of Oxford friends that included Tolkien and called itself the Inklings. Barfield's seminal work *Poetic Diction* was the outgrowth of his exploration into the function of language as developing human consciousness from a primal unity in which one word could express a cluster of inter-related perceptions – what we might now call metaphoric – to an increasingly fragmented but commensurately more precise vocabulary in which each narrower word further refined and isolated meaning. A development, we might say, from the language of poetry to the language of science.

Barfield was part of a current of philosophical thought taking shape in the early and mid 20th century. In 1925 the German philosopher Ernst Cassirer posited in *Sprache und Mythos* (translated into English as *Language and Myth*) that "[a]ll theoretical cognition takes its departure from a world already pre-formed by language" (Cassirer 1946:28), and that "the difference between [...] languages [...] is not a matter of different sounds, but of different world conceptions" (Cassirer 1946:31). "Each language" he said, "draws a magic circle round the people to whom it belongs, a circle from which there is no escape save by stepping out of it into another" (Cassirer 1946:9).

In the late 20s, 30s and 40s of the 20th century the idea was further explored by Edward Sapir and Benjamin Lee Whorf, both of them linguists, anthropologists, and philosophers (though Whorf's day-job was as an inspector for an insurance company), who over the course of those decades developed what has come to be known as the Sapir-Whorf hypothesis: the proposition that the traditional stories of a culture – its history, precepts and concepts as encoded in its language – determines the speakers' cognition of their experienced world. We know our environment through the words that create our perceptions of it. From this it followed logically that different languages containing different words for the "same" things would encode different perceptions and thus would create different realities, different worlds.

All these men, Barfield, Cassirer, Sapir, Whorf and Tolkien, were pursuing the same line of thought, that language is as much the creator of phenomena as it is the response to them. It was Tolkien, however, who put these ideas to work by using them to create his world of Middle-earth. Closest to him in time and place, it was Barfield's work that had the most influence on Tolkien, who said of Barfield's concept of original semantic unity that it had modified his whole outlook on language (Carpenter 1979:42). Not re-directed it, let us note, but modified, perhaps refined it. Tolkien was already going in the same direction, but Barfield gave him a push. In his later years Tolkien was a philosopher of language, as his more explicitly theoretical, post-*Lord of the Rings* writings coming from the 60s of the last century show. In those years he was moving, we might say, from the language of poetry to the language of science. But in his creative period, the years that gave us *The Silmarillion* and *The Hobbit* and *The Lord of the Rings*, he worked on the principle that poetry and science were not "opposite poles" but parts of the same thing. What he called his "scientifically deduced" invented languages were integrally related to his passion for myth and fairy tale (*Letters* no. 131).

The fairy-story essay, of course, enters fairly late in the game, for by 1939 Tolkien had already been putting these principles into practice in his fiction for twenty years, beginning with the "Lost Tales" that became *The Silmarillion* and continuing into *The Hobbit* and *The Lord of the Rings*. He began with a paradigm somewhat more robust than Sapir-Whorf (but still open to question), the hypothesis that a Proto-Indo-European language was the ancestor of a dispersed and divergent "family" of modern and archaic Indo-European languages (excluding Finnish, Hungarian, Estonian, and Basque). This gave him the model for his Elves and their primitive Proto-Elvish language, from which descended a dozen or so Elven languages, chief of which are Quenya and Sindarin.

But Tolkien did more than model the Indo-European language theory; he dramatized it. Starting with proto-Elven Qenya ("speech") he divided his Quendi (Speakers) and their languages by a linguistic and geographic and ultimately political fragmentation and dispersal into linguistic and cultural/political subgroups. Out of the original Quendi came, set off by prefixes, the Calaquendi (Light-elves) and the Moriquendi (Dark-elves); from the Calaquendi came the

Vanyar (Fair-elves), the Noldor (Wise-elves), the Teleri (Late-comers), while the Moriquendi acquired a variety of sub-names such as Avari (Unwilling), Úmanyar (Non-Aman), and Sindar (Grey-elves). These are all names for perceptions of and by self and other, and as those perceptions grew and changed through experience so did the names.

Elven migration is a macro rather than a micro example. A closer look at some individual names and experiences from the many Tolkien scattered so lavishly throughout *The Lord of the Rings* will show how he intended the name-thing partnership to work. I will cite examples of different ways Tolkien saw it working, examples that trace an arc from a pre-verbal period through the development, decline, and even disappearance of words over time. My first example will illustrate how the nature of the thing imposes limitations on the word. My second example will show how experience and word interconnect and develop each other. The third example will demonstrate how changed experience can keep the word but obscure the usage. My fourth example will show how time can shorten both shape and sound, and in so doing erode the meaning. And the last example will illustrate dramatically how the disappearance of the thing can deprive the language of the word.

I will start with some lines of dialogue I think everyone will recognize. In Chapter VII of Book One of *The Lord of the Rings*, "In the House of Tom Bombadil", Frodo, apologizing for what he fears might be a "foolish" question, asks Goldberry, "who is Tom Bombadil?" (*LotR* FR.I.vii). Now this is not a "foolish" question at all. It is in fact a very good question both within the fiction, where the Hobbits are understandably puzzled by the appearance of this extraordinary creature, and external to it, where readers are equally puzzled. It is one of the most Frequently Asked Questions on *Lord of the Rings* in chat rooms and posts, and one that my students have been asking me for thirty years. Goldberry's answer to Frodo's question, "He is", has misled many readers to relate her two words to the biblical "I am" and take them for an allusion to God. Careful reading and observance of the comma after "is" show that they are not, for both Goldberry and the sentence continue with what Tolkien explained in a letter was "the correct answer" (*Letters* no. 153). This is "He is, as you have seen him". Tom is *sui generis*. He is a noun that does not take a modifier. Goldberry adds ("as a concession", says Tolkien; *Letters* no. 153) a statement of *what* Tom is: "He is the Master of wood, water, and hill." Tolkien's word "concession" suggests Goldberry can see that Frodo is not quite up to the metaphysic of unique existence.

Not only that, he misunderstands her use of the word "Master", confusing it with domination and possession. "Then all this strange land belongs to him?" he asks. "No indeed!" she answers emphatically. "The trees and the grasses and all things growing or living in the land belong each to themselves. Tom Bombadil is Master." She does not explain what she means; she simply repeats the key word, *Master*. For clarification we must go again to Tolkien's *Letters*, where he writes that, "He [Tom] is *master* in a peculiar way: he has no fear and no desire of possession or domination at all" (*Letters* no. 153). It seems clear that Tolkien is using the word in the sense of "authority" or "teacher", its original Latin usage (definition #10 in the *OED*: "a teacher, a tutor, preceptor"). That says *what* but not *who*, and does not answer Frodo's question.

A few pages on in that same chapter, Frodo, trying again to get a straight answer, asks Tom directly, "Who are you, Master?" Like many good teachers, Tom answers the question with a question: "Don't you know my name yet? That's the only answer." Tolkien explained in a letter that "Goldberry and Tom are referring to the mystery of *names*" (*Letters* no. 153), though we must admit that referring to something as a "mystery" is not much of an explanation. The mystery deepens at the Council of Elrond (*LotR* FR.II.ii), where Tom acquires several additional names that also say *what* but not *who* he is. Elrond calls him Iarwain Ben-adar, "oldest and fatherless", a literal translation of Noldorin/Sindarin *iarwain* "old-young" (Hammond and Scull 2005:128), and *pen/ben* "without" + *adar* "father". The Dwarves call him Forn, which is an actual Icelandic word: *forn*, "old" in the sense of ancient past. Men of the North call him Orald (cp. German *uralt* "immemorial, hoary, very old"). In his "Guide to the Names in *The Lord of the Rings*" Tolkien noted that "*Forn* is actually the Scandinavian word for '(belonging to) ancient (days)', and *Orald* is an Old English word for 'very ancient'" (Hammond and Scull 2005:128).

Since all of these words express essentially the same idea, it seems clear that Tom's additional names add only a common acknowledgment of age to our knowledge of who he is. But "is", as in Goldberry's initial statement, is the operative word. As the oldest being, Tom comes before history and therefore cannot be related to or associated with anything but himself, his own existence. Tom is pre-language therefore not formed by it, saying of himself, "Tom was here before the river and the trees; Tom remembers the first raindrop and the first acorn. He made paths before the Big People, and saw the Little People arriving. […] Tom knew the dark under the stars when it was fearless – before the Dark Lord [not Sauron but Melkor] came from Outside" (*LotR* FR.I.vii). Like Väinämöinen, the "eternal singer" of the Finnish *Kalevala*, Tom is his world's oldest sentient being. He is fatherless, self-begotten, pre-existent. He simply "is".

Having given an answer that penetrates the mystery but does not explain it, Tom then turns Frodo's own question back on him. "Tell me, who are you, alone, yourself and nameless?" (*LotR* FR.I.vii). Without his name Frodo is not just "nameless"; he is "alone", solitary, lacking any point of reference. For contrast we can look at Bilbo's introduction of himself to Smaug in *The Hobbit* as he recites his multiple identity-conferring names: clue-finder, web-cutter, stinging fly, and (moving to upper case) Ringwinner, Luckwearer, and Barrel-rider (*H* XII). It is clear to the reader that in his own estimation Bilbo has come a long way from Gloin's description of "a little fellow bobbing and puffing on the mat" back in Bag End (*H* I). These names are performative, describing actions arising out of specific situations. Bilbo's new names are what he is and that is not who he used to be. They are what he *does*. While Smaug cautions the cocky, self-promoting Hobbit not to let his imagination (we might say his developing ego) run away with him, the idea seems to be that there is an umbilical connection between word and thing (or person), and that each in a sense creates the other.

My second example comes from one of Tolkien's most profound commentators on language, Treebeard the Ent, who carries the interconnection of name and experience several steps further. First he tells Merry and Pippin to be more cautious about letting out their "own right names". This follows the ancient notion that the connection between the name and the thing means that possession of one brings with it power over the other (which is Bilbo's real reason for all those hyphenated epithets in his conversation with Smaug). Next the old Ent announces that he is not going to tell the Hobbits *his* name because it would take too long. His name is "growing all the time", he says because it is "like a story" (*LotR* TT.III.iv). In fact, it is a story, and as such is a perfect illustration of the idea that language, mind, and story-telling are parts of the same whole. The Entish language is agglutinative, meaning that words which are actually long phrases and whole sentences can be formed by adding a cluster of suffixes to a base word. We have only a few examples, one of which is *a-lalla-lalla-rumba-kamanda-lind-or-burúmë*, which Treebeard explains (it is not really a translation) as "the thing we are standing on, where I stand and look out on fine mornings, and think about the Sun, and the grass beyond the wood, and the horses, and the clouds, and the unfolding of the world" (*LotR* TT.III.iv).

Pippin's zippy one-word translation, "hill", and Merry's suggestions of "shelf" or "step" are good for a laugh in the dynamic of the scene, but they underscore the difference in perception that for Tolkien is the basis of differences in language. The Hobbits are "hasty" folk, little in stature, quick in speech, and their language (for all that Tolkien explained their vocabulary as translation into the Common Speech) matches their personality. "Frightfully treeish" (*LotR* TT.III.iv) is Merry's two-word description of Fangorn Forest. Treebeard's extended term encompasses a world of perception over time, his experience of the hill, the weather, his response to sun, grass, horses, clouds, and the "unfolding of the world" to his perceiving eyes. We can say with some truth that Ents and Hobbits live in different worlds, or that the world "unfolds" to their eyes in different ways. The Ents' language, like the trees themselves, is slow-growing, developing over time; it has a core like a tree's heartwood to which rings are added year by year as the tree grows.

But the process has its opposite in the history of the world of Middle-earth, for language can diminish as well as grow, it can cast off as well as accumulate. This leads me and Treebeard to my third example, which involves the original, full name for what readers of *The Lord of the Rings* know as Lórien or Lothlórien, *Laurelindórenan lindelorendor malinornélion ornemalin*. Tolkien's linguistic treatment of the name and its relation to its referent, the Elven stronghold of Galadriel and Celeborn, illustrate both the agglutinative linguistic principle and its opposite process, an ongoing shortening and limitation of expression, removal rather than accretion. The full name means, "the valley where the trees in a golden light sing musically, a land of music and dreams, there are yellow trees there, it is a tree-yellow land" (*Letters* no. 230). Unlike the word for "hill", it is Entish only in structure and perception; the words themselves are Quenya. The shortened form, *Laurelindórenan* means "Land of the Valley of the Singing Gold", while the even shorter name, *Lóthlorien*, a Quenya-Sindarin hybrid, translates as "Dreamflower". *Lórien*, the name by which it is best known and most often referred to in *The Lord of the Rings*, is shorter still. It means simply "Dream", the proper name of Lórien the Vala of dreams, and as such is inevitably opposed to "waking", which we can read as "reality".

This progressive shrinking of the name becomes an indicator of Lórien's regressively receding relationship to Time and Change. Lórien is out of time in both senses of that expression. Its proper time has run out so that in the natural course of history it would have decayed. But it has not; it is outside of Time, artificially preserved, the experience of time slowed almost to a standstill by Galadriel's elven ring. "Perhaps they are right", says Treebeard, "maybe it is fading, not growing." He adds, "They are falling rather behind the world in there, I guess" (*LotR* TT.III.iv). He is right. Lórien is falling behind the times, slipping backward into the past. From his perspective on the Great River of Time Frodo sees it "like a bright ship masted with enchanted trees", a "living vision of that which has already been left far behind by the flowing stream of Time" (*LotR* TT.II.viii).

Looking forward rather than backward, Appendix F of *The Lord of the Rings* supplies the literal translation of another of Treebeard's names for Lórien: Quenya *Taurelilómëa-tumbalemorna Tumbaletaurëa Lómëanor*, which Tolkien translates literally as "Forestmanyshadowed-deepvalleyblack Deepvalleyforested Gloomyland", and paraphrases loosely as "there is a black shadow in the deep dales of the forest" (*LotR* App F.I). Here the process of naming becomes almost predictive, a foreshadowing of what will become of Lórien in the course of time. Worth noting here are the comments Tolkien made in some of his letters about the Elves and Lórien. He called his Elves "embalmers" trying to stop change (*Letters* no. 154), "as if a man were to hate a very long book still going on, and wished to settle down in a favourite chapter" (*Letters* no. 181).

The operative – and damning – term, of course, is "embalmers", with its clear connotations of preserving the appearance of life in the face of death, holding on to something when its time has passed. It is significant, I think, that these explanations are not within the work itself, but external to it. While they are derived from it, they are subsequent to it and in a completely different mode. They cannot be part of it, for they would destroy what they explained. My point is that the most dramatic conveyance of what time is doing to Lórien comes through the succession of words Tolkien used to describe, not to explain it, words intended to show process, to picture time in action.

My fourth example involves the somewhat puzzling episode in which Gandalf misinterprets the inscription on the Doors of Moria, *pedo mellon a minno*, as "Speak, friend, and enter". After faithfully and fruitlessly following these instructions he suddenly arrives at the correct reading, "Say 'Friend' and enter", without any visible clue, his only explanation being that, "Merry, of all people, was on the right track" (*LotR* FR.II.iv). Merry was the only one of the company to ask what the words meant, and the key is that the same sentence can be susceptible of different meanings, an insight that anticipates Derrida and deconstruction by several decades. In Gandalf's two successive Common Speech (English) translations, this difference is conveyed by changes in punctuation, the commas surrounding the word "friend" in the first translation suggesting that it is direct address, their removal in the second turning the word "Friend" into a password. The attendant shift from "Speak" to "Say" (words often interchangeable) underscores the slipperiness of language and its dependence on context for meaning. "Those were happier times," says Gandalf, contrasting the past when the words were inscribed and Dwarves and Elves were on better terms, with the story's present "suspicious days" (*LotR* FR.II.iv).

My final example comes from *The Hobbit* and gives us another illustration of Tolkien's philosophy of language, that loss of the thing leads to loss of the experience of the thing, and consequently to loss of the words for both thing and experience. Tolkien actually referred to this example (again obliquely and without explanation) in a letter to C.A. Furth of Allen and Unwin:

> The only philological remark (I think) in *The Hobbit* is [...] an odd mythological way of referring to linguistic philosophy, and a point that will (happily) be missed by any who have not read Barfield (few have) and probably by those who have. (*Letters* no. 15)

This occurs in Chapter XII of *The Hobbit*, "Inside Information", and describes Bilbo's reaction, both emotional and physical, to his first sight of the dragon. "To say that Bilbo's breath was taken away is no description at all. There are no words left to express his staggerment since Men changed the language that they learned of Elves in the days when all the world was wonderful" (*H* XII).

The reference to Barfield is explicit evidence that Tolkien had taken Barfield's ideas to heart and to paper. Moreover, it is worth noting that Tolkien has had to invent a new word, "staggerment", to express what there are "no words left to express". Both the nonce-word and the linguistic deficiency for which it cannot compensate result from the fact that what produced the lost words – the visceral shock produced by catching sight of a dragon in all his fearsome glory – is no longer available to the dragon-deprived experience of Men in these degenerate modern times.

In his ground-breaking essay "*Beowulf*: The Monsters and the Critics" Tolkien wrote:

> The significance of a myth is not easily to be pinned on paper by analytical reasoning [pace Sapir, Whorf, Cassirer, even Barfield]. It is at its best when it is presented by a poet who feels rather than makes explicit what his theme portends, who presents it incarnate in the world of history and geography, as our poet has done. (*MC* 15)

What Tolkien praised the poet for doing in *Beowulf* he has himself done in *The Lord of the Rings* and *The Hobbit*. Rather than make explicit, he has felt, and in so doing has made his audience feel the significance of his myth, illustrating rather than explaining what his theme portends and presenting it incarnate with its own history and geography in his world of Middle-earth.

To sum up: in Tolkien's work mythology is language and language is mythology and both are dynamic and ongoing processes. He was a practitioner, not a theorist. Tom Bombadil, Treebeard the Ent, Lórien/Lothlórien, Merry

Brandybuck, and Bilbo Baggins, each in a different way practices language as process, showing:

- how the thing imposes limitations on the word (Tom);
- how words and meanings assemble themselves over time (Treebeard);
- how both word and meaning can disassemble themselves over time, shrinking as things change (or in the case of Lórien resist change);
- how the same words in the same order can convey different meanings (Merry); and
- how loss of the thing results in loss of the word (Bilbo).

Many more examples can be found throughout the books, but I hope these have provided evidence that in the end, Tolkien's philosophy was grounded in his practice, in his words, just as his practice, his words, were the vehicle for his philosophy.

About the Author

VERLYN FLIEGER is Professor Emerita of English at the University of Maryland where she teaches courses on Tolkien, medieval and modern literature, and comparative mythology. She has written three books on Tolkien: *Splintered Light*, *A Question of Time*, and *Interrupted Music*. She has also edited a critical edition of *Smith of Wootton Major* and, together with Douglas A. Anderson, an expanded edition of "On Fairy-stories". Most recently, her collected essays have been published under the title *Green Suns and Faerie*.

Secondary Literature

BARFIELD, Owen. 1973. *Poetic Diction*. Middletown, CN: Wesleyan University Press.

CARPENTER, Humphrey. 1979. *The Inklings*. Boston: Houghton Mifflin.

CASSIRER, Ernst. 1946. *Language and Myth*. New York: Dover Publications.

HAMMOND, Wayne and Christina SCULL. 2005. *The Lord of the Rings: A Readers' Companion*. Boston: Houghton Mifflin.

Works by J.R.R. Tolkien

H: *The Hobbit: or, There and Back Again*, ed. Douglas A. Anderson. London: HarperCollins, 2001.

Letters: *The Letters of J.R.R. Tolkien*, ed. Humphrey Carpenter, with the assistance of Christopher Tolkien. London: George Allen & Unwin, 1981.

LotR: *The Lord of the Rings*. 50th anniversary edition. Boston: Houghton Mifflin, 2004.

MC: *The Monsters and the Critics and Other Essays*, ed. Christopher Tolkien. London: George Allen & Unwin, 1983.

TOFS: *Tolkien On Fairy-stories*, ed. Verlyn Flieger and Douglas A. Anderson. London: HarperCollins, 2008.

Andrea Monda & Wu Ming 4[1]

Tolkien the Catholic Philosopher?

Tolkien the Catholic writer, not philosopher

Andrea Monda

When I found out that the subject of this debate would be "Tolkien as a Catholic Philosopher", my initial response was to quip: "Well, Tolkien was definitely Catholic. But as for a philosopher? I don't know, maybe not..." Let me try to explain my reasoning.

While I have no doubts about Tolkien's Catholic faith, I am far less certain of his role as a thinker, a philosopher. Perhaps I overreach, seeing that the writer's own children, John and Priscilla Tolkien, who evidently knew him very well, decided to conclude *The Tolkien Family Album* with a photograph of their father smiling with a caption that reads: "The Laughing Philosopher".[2] It is a nickname that dates back to the Ancient Greek philosopher Democritus, and which has been recycled more recently for figures such as Chesterton and Tolkien. Now neither Chesterton nor Tolkien are philosophers, but they are both cheerful people, not only in their photos but in their literary works, and they are both, in the end, English Catholics. I will try to address this Christian joy later, as it seems to me an important factor in understanding Tolkien, a writer who, I repeat, I hesitate to call a "thinker" or "philosopher".

If it is true that Priscilla defined him as such, it is also true that she gave a very effective description of "Tolkien's method" which, in my opinion, offers irrefutable evidence to the contrary. I refer to a letter she sent me on 1st December 2004 in response to my question of whether her father ever expressed particular attention to the dogma of the Holy Trinity (I was convinced that the title of

---

1 The text of Wu Ming 4 © 2013 by Wu Ming 4. Published by arrangement with Roberto Santachiara Literary Agency.
2 See Tolkien 1992.

the third chapter in *LotR* Book I, "Three is Company" was no accident). In response, she wrote:

> I don't remember his reflections on the Trinity, either in his writing or his remarks made in my presence. [...] Though I am profoundly aware of my father's piety and faith, I do not remember him ever intent on speaking of dogma or doctrines in intellectual or abstract terms. In fact, I do not think it was ever in his heart to write or speak of religion didactically: his mode was to express religious themes and moral questions through the medium of story-telling, as in the case of "Leaf by Niggle".

I was looking for a simple response on the particulars of a chapter title (and on this point, I was left frustrated: "Three is Company," explained Priscilla, is a play on words in reference to the old English expression, "two's company, three's a crowd") but what I got instead was an exceptional insight into the writer's style, a style which recalls Christ's, who was not a moral teacher or a philosopher, but above all a great storyteller (I am referring to the more than fifty parables which fill the pages of the Gospels). Storytelling is the means by which Tolkien expresses religious themes and moral questions: he does this by telling a story where, as you will see in the second part of this debate, the humble and the last topple the proud and the powerful, where these same little people love to tell and to sing stories. Brunetto Salvarani (2004:88) writes:

> To narrate does not mean limiting oneself to accumulating anecdotes. It has critical effects, it is dangerous, it is not easy, it forces us to put ourselves at risk, to take a position, to enter the stories being told and ask what they mean. Story-telling is the typical experience of the lowly (in the Gospels' sense) and the oppressed who seek to reach freedom.[3]

Tolkien expressed his profound Catholic faith not only in his private life but also in his literary works and his masterpiece, a romance wherein, like Jesus's parables which do not speak of God directly, the "religious element is absorbed into the story and the symbolism." You will have recognized here a part of the quotation from Tolkien in which he defines his work as Catholic in the now famous letter to Father Murray from 8th December 1953:

> *The Lord of the Rings* is of course a fundamentally religious and Catholic work; unconsciously so at first, but consciously in the revision. That is why I have not

---

3 All translations are, unless otherwise indicated, by the authors.

put in, or have cut out, practically all references to anything like "religion", to cults or practices, in the imaginary world. For the religious element is absorbed into the story and the symbolism. (*Letters* no. 142)

I would like to clarify the two points just touched on: the first is that there is a kind of link between the work and the life of an author, a connection never precisely defined but which nevertheless has value; and the second is that it is typical for the Christian style to prefer a narrative dimension over abstract speculation.

As for the first point, regarding the rapport between an author's life and work, I would like to quote the philosopher Luigi Pareyson, who in his essay "I problemi attuali dell'estetica" asserts that:

> In the making of art, not only does the artist not renounce his own worldview and moral convictions, his utilitarian intent, he actually introduces them, implicitly or explicitly, into his work, they are taken in without being negated, and, if the work is successful, their very presence is converted into an active and intentional contribution to the work's artistic value, and the evaluation of the work requires that they be taken into account. (Pareyson 1987, vol. IV, 1833-835)

Across the ocean Leif Enger, one of the most interesting American writers of the last few years, wonders:

> I do not know if it's possible to write a book without your faith appearing. [...] Your faith, I think, always has something to do with the way in which you see the world, and given that my way of seeing things is Christian, this is the way in which my work should be read. Having said this, however, my book is not an attempt at evangelization. [...] If someone writes a book assuring that no element of his faith could enter into the work, what kind of book would it be? I don't think it would be a romance. Maybe a math book. (Spadaro 2009:53)

The Lord of the Rings is not a math book, nor is it a philosophy book. It was written by a man whose way of seeing things was Catholic. An accusation made toward my reading of the story is that it relies too much on Tolkien's letters, and in effect my essay can be considered a reading of Tolkien through and with the author's help, with one caveat: in his numerous and often marvellous letters, I read Tolkien reading himself, not the biographical details of his private life. In those letters it is Tolkien reading his own work from the inside out, recounting the genesis of the work while he labours on it; an epistolary critic, essentially, an indispensable treasure in beginning to understand this incredibly rich and varied story.

The second point relates to the fact that Tolkien, precisely because he is Catholic, is a writer, a narrator more than a philosopher. This is not to say that there is an opposition between philosophy and religion, faith and reason, quite the contrary (this conference was organized by the Institute which studies the greatest genius of the West, the highest peak in a time of philosophy and theology), but the point is that Christian religion is the religion of the incarnation, of concreteness, and it is based on a book, the Bible, which in accordance with Jewish mentality evades every abstract category, privileging physicality and dynamic action over fixed ideas.

Of all the artistic disciplines perhaps literature is the most "incarnate", as Flannery O'Connor said, and therefore there is a connection between Christianity and literature. Chesterton, speaking about Saint Thomas Aquinas, observed this closeness between Catholicism and romance (centred around the element of free will) and the very same O'Connor called herself a "Thomist slob", declaring that: "I write the way I do because (not though) I am a Catholic [...] because I am a Catholic, I cannot afford to be less than an artist."[4] Again Chesterton observed that man was really different from all the others: because s/he was not only a creature, but a creator, something that cannot be said of any other creature but man (Chesterton 2008:47). Finally we come to Tolkien, whose doctrine of Mythopoesis and Sub-creation is fundamental to an understanding of his poetics: "We make still by the law in which we're made" (*TL* 55). In other words: man is a creature of God and, like God the creator, man also creates, not on a primary level, but a secondary one. The artist is therefore a Sub-creator who, employing his imagination, reveals the divine light which inhabits him and from which he captures his most profound and inalienable dignity.

Although this theory is fundamental to understanding the mystery of Tolkien and his work, I will not dwell on it at length. Perhaps the point is the one made by the theologian Hans Urs von Balthasar who, referring to Hopkins, makes a general observation on the "English theological tradition which, unlike conti-

---

4 The American writer talked about these topics many times, see especially O'Connor (2001:26).

nental philosophy, has never had a conflict between image and concept, myth and revelation, intuition of God in nature and in the history of salvation" (von Balthasar 1978:8). It is as if the English people (of which Tolkien is a proud part) have a natural, untormented approach to both Logos and Mythos. Perhaps this naturalness, present in Tolkien's fiction as well, is what causes a disorienting effect in continental readers, who end up squabbling over his work, each wanting to appropriate it toward his own interests.

But I will say no more on this matter, because I want to underline a point that Jewish wisdom has already brought to light when, commenting on the passage in Isaiah 55, 8-9, the proverb "Man thinks, and God laughs," was coined. That is to say: Tolkien, Chesterton, and O'Connor – three great Catholic writers – were very intelligent people, capable of formidable philosophizing, but they were writers first and foremost, and in this they followed their model and teacher, Jesus, who did not formulate moral doctrines or present his listeners with philosophical theories, but rather churned out, one after another, beautiful and poignant narratives, the stories told in his parables. These are stories which, according to Boris Pasternak, "practically gave birth to man, common man, man as we know him." In his masterpiece, *Doctor Zhivago*, the Russian writer claimed:

> For me the most important thing is that Christ speaks in parables taken from everyday life. [...] The ancient world ended in Rome [...] into that orgy of bad taste, in gold and marble, he came, light and clothed in light, principally human, deliberately provincial, the Galilean, and from that moment the people and the gods ceased to exist, and man was born, the carpenter, the farmer, the shepherd among his flock at sunset, the man whose name didn't sound solemn and fierce, the man generously offered to all the maternal lullabies of the world. (Pasternak 1960:58)

On this page from *Doctor Zhivago*, the coming of Christ, the God-man narrator of parables, coincides with the birth of man. Now, in the more than fifty parables of Jesus the God "character" is mostly absent, just as in *The Lord of the Rings*, which in some ways resembles a long and dense parable. This brings us to an even more difficult question, that is: if we replace Tolkien the Christian philosopher with the Christian writer, it begs the question: what does a "Christian writer" mean? Does it make more sense to speak of a Christian novelist or a Christian novel? *Vexata quaestio*, impossible to synthesize, but perhaps a few quotations can help us get started.

Take O'Connor again for example: "Fiction is about everything human and we are made out of dust, and if you scorn getting yourself dusty, then you shouldn't try to write fiction" (O'Connor 1993:42). In the same years in which O'Connor was writing her observations, Graham Greene wrote several essays on the "paradox of Christianity" along similar lines. Greene asserted:

> I belong to a group, the Catholic Church, which would present me with grave problems as a writer if I were not saved by my disloyalty. [...] Literature has nothing to do with edification. I am not arguing that literature is amoral, but that it presents a personal moral. [...] Catholic novelists (I would rather say novelists who are Catholics) should take [Cardinal] Newman as their patron. No one understood their problem better or defended them more skillfully from the attacks of piety (that morbid growth of religion). Let me copy out the passage. It really has more than one bearing on our discussion. He is defending the teaching of literature in a Catholic university: "I say, from the nature of the case, if Literature is to be made a study of human nature, you cannot have a Christian Literature. It is a contradiction in terms to attempt a sinless Literature of a sinful man. You may gather together something very great and high, something higher than any Literature ever was; and when you have done so, you will find that it is not Literature at all." (Green 1958:147)

If a character of such authority as Cardinal Newman claims not to demand Christian literature, there seems nothing else to do but tip my hat and adhere to his vision. Perhaps the Milanese writer Luca Doninelli was right when he stated that, for him, to call someone a "Catholic writer" was the same as saying "blonde or dark-haired writer".[5] Or, even better, as my friend Saverio Simonelli (2000) puts it, one must be wary of "giving in to the temptation to single out an impossible typology of Christian writers."

The aforementioned Leif Enger has something to add on the subject of Christian fiction, which he claims are those stories which "spark the need for man's true redemption [...] the books which show that man is incapable of saving himself, redeeming himself alone" (Spadaro 2009:53). It seems to me

---

5 Doninelli said this during a congress held 1 February 2000 in Rome at the "Pontificio Consiglio per la Cultura" on the topic "Literature and Catholicism in the 20th century: the poetics of faith in the century of God's death."

that this idea could easily be applied to Tolkien's masterpiece. Even if God appears to be absent, His Providence figures strongly.

The great American poet, if not exactly militant Christian, Raymond Carver points out in *No Heroics, Please* that

> in the best novels and short stories, goodness is recognized as such. Loyalty, love, fortitude, courage, integrity may not always be rewarded, but they are recognized as good or noble actions and qualities; and evil or base or simply stupid behavior is seen and held up for what it is: evil, base, or stupid behaviour. In the end, absolutes do exist in life, and we would do well not to forget it. (Carver 2002:227)

Besides seeming to defy every minimalist label ever stuck onto Carver in Italy, I must say that this quote reminds me of what Michael Tolkien said of his father's work, and of Aragorn's words. Michael said that for him there is nothing mysterious about the reason for his father's success, whose genius could not help but touch people of all ages and characters, sick and tired of ugliness, instability, borrowed values and trivial philosophies sold to them as sad substitutes for beauty, mystery, exaltation, adventure, heroism and joy, things without which man's soul becomes barren and dies within him (Grotta 1983:183-84).

Aragorn's line, on the other hand, comes from the exchange with Éomer on the plains of Rohan:

> "It is hard to be sure of anything among so many marvels. The world is all grown strange. Elf and Dwarf in company walk in our daily fields; and folk speak with the Lady of the Wood and yet live; and the Sword comes back to war that was broken in the long ages ere the fathers of our fathers rode into the Mark! How shall a man judge what to do in such times?"
> "As he ever has judged", said Aragorn. "Good and ill have not changed since yesteryear; nor are they one thing among Elves and Dwarves and another among Men. It is a man's part to discern them, as much in the Golden Wood as in his own house". (*LotR* TT.III.ii)

The connection between Catholicism and humanism is a strong one, and perhaps this is part of what makes it so difficult to define writers and stories as "Catholic"; however, we should not forget that Tolkien himself defined his work as "fundamentally religious and Catholic".

The point is that Tolkien here is not only a writer but a reader (so much so that in the famous aforementioned letter from 1953 in which he offered this definition, he underlined that the story's Catholicism was unconscious in the drafting, and only later became clear in revision, thus through re-reading). For me, this is a key point. In his essay on "Fantastic Imagination" George MacDonald, one of the fathers of modern fantasy and a teacher of Lewis and Tolkien, argues that the reader is just as important as the author, since a story exists not so much to transmit a meaning as to awaken one (MacDonald 2000:7). In his literary essays, theologian Karl Rahner also emphasizes reading over writing,[6] not to mention a poet like Borges who has always said he was more proud of the books he has read than those he has written because "man is what he reads" (Borges 1990:73). But getting back to Tolkien, in the more than four hundred letters which make up his published correspondence, there are many in which he rereads and reconstructs his work with a critical and meticulous air. Reading these letters by a writer reading himself is, for me, a mere "external" Catholic reader of Tolkien, very instructive.

To sum up: in my opinion the term "Catholic philosopher" does not fit Tolkien, and I am not sure that "Catholic writer" makes much sense either; but there surely exist Catholic *readers*, and I, on the one hand, do not intend to exhaust all the interpretive possibilities of Tolkien with my reading, though on the other I cannot deny that above all else I find in this story a rich symbolic power that enriches me not only as a reader but also as a Catholic. Therefore, I want to unravel and unfold rather than exhaust the Catholic symbolism I find in the pages of Tolkien's stories (in the characters, the narrative twists, etc.) by which my reading does not seek to be an ideological cage that closes the story within one rigid interpretation, but one which opens the text, allowing all kinds of symbolic potential to emerge. If "fiction is about everything human", as O'Connor (1993:42) said, I have to think that a Catholic has no fear of reality and therefore writes and comments on everything. As Tolkien preferred the term applicability to allegory, my reading too can be "applicable". That is: in my essays I provide a symbolic key to reading, from my own point of view, that I hope is coherent and able to unlock the beauty of the work. In addition, this symbolic reading finds support in the author's own self-analysis. Here is the question: is the reading key I provide, at the end of the day, coherent? Does it hold up? It is not the last word on Tolkien, obviously, only the "awakened"

---

6 In particular see Rahner 1964.

meaning as MacDonald would say, the resonance stemming from my Catholic conscience's reaction to this work, the recognition of its symbolism and beauty. Now the question I would ask of my interlocutor is this: Tolkien, following Christ, is not a Catholic thinker, but is he perhaps a Catholic writer? And if not, what kind of writer is he? What does Wu Ming 4 read in the pages of this great writer? What is his reading of Tolkien?

Storyteller

Wu Ming 4

It has already been said that Tolkien never explicitly cited any philosophers in his work, nor spent much time discussing philosophical theories; if anything, he used philosophical concepts to create a literary universe which mirrors the real world, and to shape its values and conflicts. This is what all writers do.

Similarly, it is possible to trace in Tolkien's work elements which evidently derive from religion. Although the creation of Arda does not rehash the Judeo-Christian cosmogony word-for-word, it is however a monotheistic universe in which an original corruption occurs, an angel falls, and the struggle between good and evil is ongoing, or in which the original light gradually splinters, becoming at times soft and at others bright. Above all, it is a world saved by little people, by small beings who become the cornerstone of the collective destiny.

One can go on and on looking for similarities and contact points between Tolkien's work and the stories of the Christian world, but none of this really answers the question: was Tolkien a Catholic philosopher?

As far as the term "philosopher" is concerned, it is clear that we must recognize that narrative choices are not made by chance or for convenience; rather, they are motivated by Tolkien's deepest thoughts and attitudes. That said, we must rephrase the question in better terms, and better understand the terms themselves in order to avoid misunderstandings and simplifications.

If then Tolkien was not a philosopher, the question becomes: was Tolkien a Catholic storyteller?

The expression "Catholic storyteller" usually refers to a writer closely bound to his faith or religion, that is, intent on putting the virtues and principles of Christianity and Catholicism into narrative form as, for example, Dante Alighieri or Alessandro Manzoni did. If this is the meaning of the question, then my response would be "no, Tolkien was not". He did not theologize through his stories, or create a Christian allegory, much less dress up Catholic ethics in the form of an epic adventure. Of course, he used Christian (as well as other) values and symbols; he was inspired by the vision of the world which he himself shared, without, however, producing a narrative architecture coherently and uniquely Christian.

We know how much he resented those who sought to read his work within a purely religious framework. Tolkien puts it well when he claims to have "deliberately written a tale which is built on or out of certain 'religious' ideas, but is *not* an allegory of them (or anything else), and does not mention them overtly, still less preach them" (*Letters* no. 283). Tolkien maintained that his narrative had no "allegorical intentions general, particular, or topical, moral, religious, or political" (*Letters* no. 165). This is why he cannot be associated with Alighieri or Manzoni, who were animated by a very different spirit. They were *engagés* writers, and they consciously constructed Christian narratives, viewing the things of this world through a religious lens. Tolkien's intent and *modus operandi* were, by his own admission, completely different. He claims to have realized that *The Lord of the Rings* is a "fundamentally religious and Catholic work [...] in the revision", but not while he was writing it (*Letters* no. 142) – thus it was so *a posteriori*, having been moved from the beginning simply by the desire to tell "an exciting story" (*Letters* no. 208).

Thus if Tolkien cannot be equated with the aforementioned authors, then, to my mind, he should not be read like them either. Moreover, the fact that the foundations of his story were Catholic does not imply that the story exhausts itself in them. On the contrary, the subtle incoherence of the big picture, the collision between Christian and other elements of inspiration, is what renders the applicability of Tolkien's work inexhaustible. Without this collision, his tales would otherwise risk being reduced to a mere translation of the message found in the Gospels – resembling the moral allegory which Tolkien so forcefully rejected.

Tom Shippey has reflected at length on these "inconsistencies" and on the subtle shifts made with regard to Christian narrative. For example, when he observes in the pages of *The Lord of the Rings* a relatively ambiguous conception of evil, oscillating between an orthodox Boethian and a heretical Manichean point of view: "Tolkien sets up a running ambivalence throughout the whole of *The Lord of the Rings*, which acts as an answer at once orthodox and questioning to the whole problem of the existence and source of evil in a universe created [...] by a benevolent God" (Shippey 2001:130). Or, when he analyses the internal eschatology of Tolkien's sub-creation, coming to the conclusion that "*The Lord of the Rings*, then, contains within it hints of the Christian message, but refuses just to repeat it. The myths of Middle-earth furthermore determinedely reject any sense of ultimate salvation" (Shippey 2001:210).

It is precisely this imbalance which keeps Middle-earth forever fertile, because it allows Tolkien's sub-creation to elude any particular theological or ideological systematization.

If, on the other hand, by "Catholic storyteller" we mean to refer to something which comes before the story, that is, something which constitutes the roots of Tolkien's narrative vocation, as Andrea Monda argues, then we are saying that Tolkien was a Catholic who wrote stories. In this sense, I also admit that Catholicism might have been a necessary condition subjectively speaking, but it was not at any rate poetically sufficient to define the scope and implications of his work.

Inspiration, more or less tied to faith, is one thing that can move an author, his poetics is another; and still another is that which the story ultimately expresses.

Inspiration, poetics, and thematic scope are three aspects that should never be superimposed lightly. To put it jokingly: reading Tolkien with *The Lord of the Rings* in one hand and his private letters in the other is a dubious exercise, because it presupposes that within a literary text there is nothing other than the author himself, his stated or latent intentions, his idiosyncrasies, and not also a stratification of imagination, narrative archetypes, images, and mythologems which extend far beyond the subjective experience of the writer. Yet only this surplus can hope to explain how Tolkien's works have obtained such an overwhelming and lasting success even in cultural contexts a long way from Catholicism and Christianity.

The above explains why I gladly leave the discussion of Tolkien's religious inspiration to biographers, and rather want to concentrate on his poetics.

In this case it is much easier (and not so haphazard) to single out the truly religious element: namely the truth in the story, the myth. For Tolkien, there exists a part of truth that is expressed through art and mythopoesis, due to the presence of the divine light in man: our myths are the misshapen reflections of true myth, originally written by the Creator. God's great gift to humanity is the ability to sub-create, the artistic ability, the deepest expression of our specific nature and a part of our very being. Artistic creativity is therefore an essential part of human nature, capable of expressing partial truths about things. While truth for the Catholic Tolkien, referring to a transcendent plane, may be far different from the Jungian's universal truth innate in the human psyche, the potential given to the sub-creative art remains central.

As Robert Graves, a celebrated contemporary of Tolkien, noted more than sixty years ago, it was the Greek philosophers of the classic age who first sanctioned the break between philosophy and poetry as distinct languages, one referring to objective, and the other to subjective reality (Graves 1992:14-15). According to Graves, there was once a time, before the Minoan era, in which art and philosophy were probably one and the same, and to know truth it was not necessary to distinguish, as Gilles Deleuze put it, "concepts" from the "percepts": they were both steps on the same path of knowledge and experience of the world (Deleuze & Guattari 1996:161-263). There, Tolkien still would have bet on poetry: he would have reversed the Platonic rapport between deductive dialogue and myth in favour of the second. And this, on a philosophical and aesthetic level, is interesting regardless of the faith that motivated him.

At any rate, as Tolkien would have said, I do not want to get mixed up with philosophers. As a storyteller with a Marxist background, I am interested in retracing in his poetics not so much the connection between narrative and expression of truth, as that between narrative and transformation of reality.

And as a storyteller *tout court* I can do so only through analysis of the literary text. But not before leaving the next word to my interlocutor.

Little Hobbits: Tolkien's great invention

Andrea Monda

Before moving on to the second point of our debate, I would like to clarify two small points in response to Wu Ming 4's interesting observations. The first regards his definition of Dante and Manzoni as Catholic writers in the strictest sense, a remark which does not wholly convince me. I keep thinking like Greene (who cites in his defence Cardinal Newman, as I mentioned before) that the "disloyalty", which here is synonymous with "freedom", is that which characterizes the writer who is also Catholic. Belonging to the Church is not like being a part of a political party. Dante and Manzoni demonstrate this clearly: the first is sufficiently in conflict with the ecclesiastic institution that he lives the second part of his life in exile far from his family and his city (he even stirs up quite a controversy by tossing the reigning Pope Boniface VIII into the circles of Hell), while for the latter there has been an ongoing debate concerning the nature of his Catholicism, which some Catholic scholars have downplayed or even denied, as is the case in the Milanese journal "Catholic Studies".

The second unconvincing point is my colleague's incipit, when he says: "if anything, he [Tolkien] used philosophical concepts to create a literary universe which mirrors the real world, and to shape its values and conflicts. This is what all writers do." Here, too, I beg to differ. Oscar Wilde is more convincing when he says that "the sculptor thinks in marble." Otherwise, anyone who wants to say something would be a philosopher; but the task is completed with the help of many different means: with pen, marble, or brush... Perhaps it is actually the reverse: artists "make" something which then speaks, revealing different things to different people, though perhaps many of these things are unknown to the artists themselves.

But let us move on to the second point of our discussion: the role and importance of Hobbits, where perhaps we will find that my colleague and I are in agreement. It was Wu Ming 4 himself who on many occasions has underlined the fact that Tolkien's tale is one of overcoming the Northern theory of courage, in which heroism is no longer the prerogative of the chosen elite, but of the smallest and the last.[7] On this I have very little to add.

But before speaking of the small, I'd like to say something about the big – the giants. I will read you two brief quotes:

> There were giants in the earth in those days, and also after that, when the sons of God came in unto the daughters of men, and they bore sons to them, the same became mighty men who were of old, men of renown. (Gn 6:1-8)

> The land, through which we have gone through to spy it out, is a land that eats up its inhabitants; and all the people that we saw in it are men of a great stature. And there we saw giants, the sons of Anak, of the race of the giants; and we were in our own sight as locusts, and so we were in their sight. (Nm 13:32-33)

These two quotes are taken neither from Tolkien nor from pagan legends, but from the Bible. Reading only these two lines we might say that the Bible, too, is a pagan text. Abraham, the father of all believers, was pagan too, and until Moses there was still no full affirmation of monotheism. The point is that Judaism and later Christianity come after and encompass paganism (not viceversa). Obviously paganism contains profound truths about man which are not lost or erased by the advent of Christianity. Perhaps an architectural example can be of service: the columns of the Christian basilicas often derive from pagan temples, but they are inserted into a Christian architectural plan. We find something similar in Tolkien's story. *The Silmarillion* is full of giants (Valar, Maiar, Balrogs, and so on) and "pagan" stories (even if they are included in a cosmogonical vision very similar to Genesis) and it is an Elf-centric saga, while *The Lord of the Rings* is Hobbit-centric,[8] which is, in my opinion, Christian. If the story had Men or Elves at its centre, Tolkien "the philosopher" might have emerged more, but instead we have Hobbits, who, at most, arrive at the speculative conclusion that "tales never end" (*LotR* TT.IV.viii) – one of the

---

7 See Wu Ming 4's *L'eroe imperfetto* and his "Prefazione" in *Il ritorno di Beorhtnoth figlio di Beorhthelm*.
8 We find this concept in many letters written by Tolkien, especially letter no. 181.

story's "topical" moments – but drop the reflection immediately because they are living the story, not vivisecting it. Hobbits are more active than reflective, and even if their favourite pastime often coincides with the pleasures of leisure, some are ready to be torn from their idleness to answer the "call". Ready to set off, these "revolutionary and transgressive" Hobbits (daring to pass the borders of the Shire and enter the world outside, wild and dangerous) are clearly the main protagonists both of *The Hobbit* and *The Lord of the Rings*, to the extent that the reader discovers the lands of Middle-earth by tracing their steps. Like guides, they introduce us to the ancient forest of Fangorn (Merry and Pippin), the gardens of Ithilien (Sam and Frodo), the plains of Rohan (Merry), the high towers of Gondor (Pippin), and finally the desolate land of Mordor (Sam and Frodo again, guided by that strangest of Hobbits, Sméagol). It is interesting to note that the only place in which the Hobbits do not set foot is the Paths of the Dead. Because Hobbits are alive, *the living* in a disappearing world of an undeniably pagan flavour: it is no accident that Tolkien does not show us the Paths of the Dead "live" but only through the brief, *ex post facto* account of Gimli and Legolas.

Tolkien was undoubtedly a careful and able "director" of the *mis-en-scene*, rightly placing the camera behind the shoulders of these little but lively Halflings as the story unfolds from beginning to end, when all the travellers have returned home (some ready to depart again). "The readiness is all", Hamlet says (*Hamlet*, Act 5, Scene 2), and this is perhaps the chief virtue of Hobbits, because they have nothing else but the tenacity with which to resist and guard that which grows and has roots in the earth. They too seem to have strong roots in the earth, they are Halflings, "Half-grown hobbits, the hole-dwellers" (*LotR* TT.III.iv) as is clarified in Fangorn forest in front of Treebeard himself, the great cataloguer. If the 20th century opens with the prophecy of the death of God and the advent of the superman, Tolkien responds midway through with the birth of the Halflings, the only ones capable of winning the battle for existence. Hobbits are the obvious protagonists of the story, always in the heart of the action, and this centrality is in my opinion the proof of the Catholic fabric of which Tolkien's masterpiece is made. Their arriving in the midst of the War of the Ring wreaks havoc, overturns fortunes and blows up predetermined patterns. The Hobbits are the agents of the Gospel mystery, that of the beatitudes by which the last shall be first and the first shall be they, these little men who arrive last and enter the scene of Tolkien's invented world, ensuring that wherever they tread the revolution of humility will follow.

"And neither strength nor wisdom will carry us far upon it. This quest may be attempted by the weak with as much hope as the strong. Yet such is oft the course of deeds that move the wheels of the world: small hands do them because they must, while the eyes of the great are elsewhere" (*LotR* FR.II. ii). These are the words with which Elrond recognizes that his original plan for the Company is no longer valid and therefore includes four Hobbits in the group of nine. But the other giants of Middle-earth must also take these newcomers into account:

- Galadriel must also welcome the Hobbits, and her greatest gift will be that which she saves for Frodo and Sam (the only ones who look into her Mirror).
- Gandalf and Saruman, the powerful wizards, will struggle with this new and apparently insignificant people, from the first to the last page of the story. The only difference is that Gandalf recognizes their hidden greatness, and he himself, the *smaller* of the two, will in the end become the greater, taking Saruman's place and distinctive colour, moving from the melancholy and modest grey (recalling Cinderella) to the splendour of white.
- Théoden will take Merry as squire and show him great kindness, while Denethor commands Pippin somewhat roughly. The rule of reversals goes for this case as well, as the *lesser* of the two old sovereigns grows and becomes greater, while the Steward of Gondor ends tragically in a desperate act of suicide.
- Faramir and Boromir, Denethor's sons, will both have to deal with Frodo and the Ring, but with very different motives and outcomes. Once again, the *lesser* surpasses the greater.

These are all stories with an unmistakably biblical flavour: Cain and Abel, Isaac, Jacob and Isaiah and then Joseph and David. The whole story of Israel is nicely summed up in the words of the Magnificat:

my spirit rejoices in God my Saviour, for he has looked with favour on his lowly servant. [...] He has shown the strength of his arm, he has scattered the proud in their conceit. He has cast down the mighty from their thrones, and has lifted up the lowly.

"The things I believed most then, the things I believe most now, are the things called fairy tales" Chesterton said in *Orthodoxy*, "They seem to me to be the entirely reasonable things. [...] Fairyland is nothing but the sunny country of common sense. [...] There is the lesson of "Cinderella", which is the same as that of the Magnificat – *exaltavit humiles*" (Chesterton 1980:68). It is the same lesson which emerges from reading *The Lord of the Rings*. In a letter explaining the origins of the story, Tolkien cites the same passage from the Magnificat:

> Since *The Hobbit* was a success, a sequel was called for; and the remote Elvish Legends were turned down [...] Anyway I myself saw the value of Hobbits, in putting earth under the feet of "romance", and in providing subjects for "ennoblement" and heroes more praiseworthy than the professionals: *nolo heroizari* is of course as good a start for a hero, as *nolo episcopari* for a bishop. Not that I am a "democrat" in any of its current uses; except that I suppose, to speak in literary terms, we are all equal before the Great Author, *qui deposuit potentes de sede et exaltavit humiles*. (*Letters* no. 163)

The moral of the story written by Tolkien would then be the exaltation of the humble Hobbits, their "sanctification"[9] or "ennoblement", to use a term dear to the writer, as frequent references in his letters make clear. In one letter from 1956, for example, Tolkien confesses his affection for his Hobbits by referring to another famous fable: "I loved them myself, since I love the vulgar and simple as dearly as the noble, and nothing moves my heart (beyond all the passions and heartbreaks of the world) so much as 'ennoblement' (from the Ugly Duckling to Frodo)" (*Letters* no. 180).[10]

I will not dwell much further on this point, though it is, I think, crucial. I decline in part because this is the subject of my latest essay (Monda 2008). The following is a brief overview:

---

9 Tolkien himself used this word, and he used also the word "ennoblement" referring to Frodo's development (*Letters* no. 181).
10 We can find references to the Hobbits' "ennoblement" process in other letters, especially nos. 165, 180 and 181.

- Hobbits are the simple, the humble, the last, the children and the smallest of the Gospel (Mt 18:1-5); the poor of the beatitudes, the *anawìm* of the Gospel of Luke, the "poor in spirit" (Dupont 1992:606).
- Faced with these lowly Hobbits, the great and proud do not bend, do not understand, and finally fall. The contrast between the simplicity of the Hobbits and the vainglory of the proud is the same that we find in the hymn of joy in the Gospel of Matthew with which Jesus gives praise to the Father because "thou hast hidden these things from the wise and understanding and revealed them to babes" (Mt 11:25).
- It is the opening to God, the readiness and willingness to respond to His call, the virtue that redeems and saves the lowly, it is their "receptiveness which does not seek assurances and does not stop to reflect on itself, for the knowledge of God, different to the point that it seems like scandal to the guide and foolishness to Gentiles (1 Cor 1:23)" (von Balthasar 1983:25).
- These lowly Hobbits, just like the ancient people of Israel, live in hiding, jealously guarding their existence apart. They have no love for external intrusions; even less for journeys to the "outside" world themselves, which would be moreover fatal for them: they would in fact be wiped out pitilessly. Because of this, they go unnoticed (by all except Gandalf and the Rangers of the North, led by Aragorn), living within the borders of their Shire. The fact that the Hobbits do not enjoy a great reputation takes up a recurrent narrative motif in the Gospels where neither Bethlehem, nor Nazareth, nor the son of a carpenter, etc. enjoy great fame initially. This is also the reason for the Hobbits's temporary safety: they are not taken into consideration by the forces of evil either, Sauron's Orcs pay little attention to this silly and innocuous race from the Northwest of Middle-earth.

If my summary holds up, it demonstrates the clear difference between Tolkien's story and the rest of so-called *heroic fantasy*: take, for example, a "classic" of this genre, the saga of the brawny Conan the Barbarian by Robert E. Howard. In this aspect Tolkien clearly runs against the mainstream of fantasy. The hero which Tolkien presents to the reader is a completely different kind of hero: a Christian one. Frodo's choice is revolutionary from any point of view, even according to the political logic of Middle-earth (that is the human world): it is the paradoxical choice of self-sacrifice. Moral, not physical strength is what counts, the opening of mind and heart. It counts to have this religious and Christian attitude: Christians, the followers of Christ, are in fact called to renounce themselves and take up the cross, "For whoever would save his life will lose it, and whoever loses his life for my sake will find it" (Mt 16:24-25). It is an attitude that joins obedience and humility and seems foolish to the eyes of the world, a kind of madness. The mission that Gandalf proposes to the Fellowship, to travel into the heart of enemy territory in order to destroy the Ring of Power, is in effect the most foolish of all, as Gandalf himself observes:

> Well, let folly be our cloak, a veil before the eyes of the Enemy! For he is very wise, and weighs all things to a nicety in the scales of his malice. But the only measure that he knows is desire, desire for power; and so he judges all hearts. Into his heart the thought will not enter that any will refuse it, that having the Ring we may seek to destroy it. (*LotR* FR.II.ii)

To this we might add Paul's message to the Corinthians: "but God chose what is foolish in the world to shame the wise, God chose what is weak in the world to shame the strong, God chose what is low and despised in the world, even things that are not, to bring to nothing things that are" (1 Cor 1:27-28). This view offers us a valuable contrast to the aforementioned figures who represent "wisdom" and "strength" and those who think that they possess the things that are, yet who will be reduced to nothing. This is Sauron's destiny: the haughty, the solitary (one tower and one eye) against which a ragtag fellowship, composed mostly of little Hobbits, fights. Sauron the greatest of the great who thinks to have the "things that are" and who will indeed be brought to nothing.

Frodo, Sam and Gollum succeed in bringing down the Dark Lord of Mordor: there could be no greater surprise or reversal. But the Gospel paradox of the story can be seen also, for example, in the comparison between Denethor and Pippin. The two are polar opposites: the Steward of Gondor is as severe and tragic as the youngest member of the Fellowship is ridiculous and clumsy.

Perhaps this pair best represents the shared presence of paganism and Catholicism within the narrative. Tolkien views paganism, and the reader with him, with a mixture of admiration, devotion, and tenderness. No one feels hate or anger toward Denethor; it is pity that prevails. Paganism is something noble, even beautiful, but unfulfilled, a plant full of promise which never came to full bloom. It was missing a leap, perhaps a pinch of madness: Greek wisdom lacked Christian paradox, as the title of Charles Moeller's famous essay goes. Nobility and aristocracy encase Denethor in a sterile and ultimately self-destructive pride, a fate which he shares with his eldest son Boromir. Perhaps it is not by chance that Faramir, possessing a sense of humility and obedience, is the one to make a gesture before the meal, highly reminiscent of a prayer, one of the few moments of explicit religiousness in the story. Facing the growing delirium of Denethor, we notice the small outline of Pippin in the background, like the Catholicism behind the whole story. It is as if to say that Catholicism is always a double-edged sword, at once a stumbling block and a chance for redemption and salvation. Denethor, Saruman, and Théoden, all stumble over these little people, but only Théoden will embrace them, and in this way he achieves a redemption which the others are excluded from on account of their pride.

I will conclude by reiterating that these Hobbits represent the great literary novelty (or should I say "the good news") which Tolkien brought to the heart of the 20th century. The rest we know already; Hobbits enter into human history and remain there for a long time. Like all great novelties, they actually recall something ancient, as I tried to demonstrate by speaking of traditional fairy stories, from Cinderella to the Ugly Duckling, and they even recall something much less remote, especially for Italians: our country's greatest novel. Who else are Hobbits but the "mechanical people and small business" of whom Manzoni speaks? At a closer look, the comparison between Manzoni and Tolkien is fitting in other ways as well. In Tolkien there is also the double level of the small story intersecting with history. The Hobbit protagonists of *The Lord of the Rings* rightly enter into history and what is more, they resolve it. In addition, the story's resolution takes place, both for Tolkien and Manzoni (both Catholics), under the sign of Providence and the intervention of Grace. I will say nothing further about Providence, seeing as Professor Shippey has already addressed it. As for Grace, which by the end of Tolkien's story also has a paradoxical and grotesque (very O'Connorian) side in Gollum, I once more direct you to my previous essay and gladly leave the next word to my interlocutor.

Between saying and doing: the poetics of narration

Wu Ming 4

One of the crucial aspects of Tolkien's poetics is found inscribed in the story itself being told, which contains clear meta-narrative comments.

At the beginning of *The Hobbit*, the omniscient narrator describes the subject of the story: "This is a story of how a Baggins had an adventure, found himself doing and saying things altogether unexpected" (*H* I). A few pages later, the same Baggins refers to the wizard Gandalf in these terms:

> Not the fellow who used to tell such wonderful tales at parties, about dragons and goblins and giants and the rescue of princesses and the unexpected luck of widow's sons? [...] Not the Gandalf who was responsible for so many quiet lads and lasses going off into the Blue for mad adventures. Anything from climbing trees to visiting Elves – or sailing in ships, sailing to other shores! (*H* I)

Adventure stories generate in young readers the desire to truly live them. A little later, Bilbo experiences himself the effects of poetry after listening to the Dwarves' song about their adventures: "Then something Tookish woke up inside him, and he wished to go and see the great mountains, and hear the pine-trees and the waterfalls, and explore the caves, and wear a sword instead of a walking-stick" (*H* I).

The stories allow us to live vicariously, to escape from ourselves and from our routines, they push us toward the Unknown, that is toward that which is other from us. Narrative therefore produces practical effects: stories can make us do things, even "unexpected" ones.

This is a theme that returns with a vengeance later in *The Lord of the Rings*. There are some moments in the novel in which the characters seem on the verge of realising that they are already participating in an epic adventure, regardless of how it ends. It is essentially a kind of reflection on the power of stories.

For example, in Chapter V of Book II, when the Fellowship is passing through the Mines of Moria, they discover the account of the fate of Balin's people. It is a diary of the Dwarf colony established in Moria, ending with a fragmentary account, worn by the years, of their last resistance against the Orcs. These are the words Gandalf reads: "We cannot get out. They have taken the Bridge and second hall. [...] We cannot get out. The end comes [...] drums, drums in the deep [...] they are coming" (*LotR* FR.II.v).

Just after the reading, the drums are heard for real, the Orcs come, and the protagonists find themselves repeating the words they have just read: "'They are coming!' cried Legolas. 'We cannot get out,' said Gimli. 'Trapped!' cried Gandalf. 'Why did I delay? Here we are, caught, just as they were before.'" (*LotR* FR.II.v). It seems almost as if the reading of the account of the last moments of the Dwarves holed up in that chamber has recreated the scene and brought it to life in the present. There is a direct connection between the story and the adventure that the protagonists are experiencing.

This connection is able not only to evoke past stories but also to allude to future events. When Aragorn, together with his two companions, decides to chase the Orcs who have taken Merry and Pippin captive, he says that the chase "shall be accounted a marvel among the Three Kindreds: Elves, Dwarves, and Men" (*LotR* TT.III.i). The hunt they are about to begin will be passed down and become legend. The same idea is picked up again when Éomer, Marshal of the Riddermark, runs into the strange trio and cannot contain his surprise, saying, "Dreams and legends spring to life out of the grass" (*LotR* TT.III.ii). Later, when he hears of the Halflings, who are to him only fairy-tale creatures, one of the Rider wonders: "Do we walk in legends or on the green earth in the daylight?" (*LotR* TT.III.ii).

But it is Aragorn's response that is most interesting: "'A man may do both,' said Aragorn. 'For not we but those who come after will make the legends of our time. The green earth, say you? That is a mighty matter of legend, though you tread it under the light of day!'" (*LotR* TT.III.ii).

Sam demonstrates the same awareness when he reflects on the relationship between his adventure and the stories which he so loves:

> The brave things in the old tales and songs, Mr. Frodo: adventures, as I used to call them. [...] Folk seem to have been just landed in them, usually – their paths were laid that way, as you put it. But I expect they had lots of chances,

like us, of turning back, only they didn't. And if they had, we shouldn't know, because they'd have been forgotten. We hear about those as just went on – and not all to a good end, mind you [...] I wonder what sort of a tale we've fallen into? (*LotR* TT.IV.viii)

He immediately realizes that in effect their own adventure is connected to the legends that they have heard sung by the Elves: "'Why, to think of it, we're in the same tale still! It's going on. Don't the great tales never end?' 'No, they never end as tales,' said Frodo. 'But the people in them come, and go when their part's ended. Our part will end later – or sooner.'" (*LotR* TT.IV.viii).

Moments later, the two Hobbits imagine themselves as characters of popular tales, sung by fathers to sons around the fireplace: "and people will say: 'Let's hear about Frodo and the Ring!' And they'll say: 'Yes, that's one of my favourite stories. Frodo was very brave, wasn't he, dad?' 'Yes, my boy, the famousest of the hobbits, and that's saying a lot.'" (*LotR* TT.IV.viii).

And again, at the very end, when all seems lost, Sam consoles himself with the thought that he may become a character in a story:

> "What a tale we have been in, Mr. Frodo, haven't we?" he said. "I wish I could hear it told! Do you think they'll say: *Now comes the story of Nine-fingered Frodo and the Ring of Doom*? And then everyone will hush, like we did, when in Rivendell they told us the tale of Beren One-hand and the Great Jewel. I wish I could hear it! And I wonder how it will go on after our part." (*LotR* RK.VI.iv)

In that moment Sam cannot know that it will be a minstrel of Gondor who sings the song after the final eucatastrophe: what he is worried about is who he can pass the story on to.

What Tolkien is suggesting through his characters' reflections is a virtuous cycle between past, present, and future which has narration at its centre. The old stories influence the present undertaking, which in turn becomes the legend of tomorrow, and so on. It is a belief strongly rooted enough that, through the device of the rediscovered manuscript, it transforms both protagonists of the Ring cycle into narrators. *The Hobbit* contains the memoirs of Bilbo Baggins, written by his own hand, after returning from his first trip; *The Lord of the Rings* those of Frodo, who, before leaving Middle-earth forever, passes on the testimony to Sam, telling him: "The last pages are for you" (*LotR* RK.VI.ix). In this way, the story passes from hand to hand and mind to mind, and with the addition of appendices, attachments, historic and ethnographic information, genealogies, timelines, etc., *The Red Book of Westmarch* is composed over time, eventually becoming a collective macro-account.

Like the Sumerian hero Gilgamesh who returns from his travels and engraves his story on clay tablets, or Lawrence of Arabia who returns to his home country to write *The Seven Pillars of Wisdom*, the hero becomes a narrator. The narrator thus finds himself in the middle of an inexhaustible flow of stories, in the deferred moment between saying and doing, between story and life. An interactive link exists between the Secondary and Primary Worlds: stories and myths can speak to the most hidden aspects of our being and push us to do completely unexpected things, to strike out for the unknown, sail to other shores. They can even transform a placid country Hobbit into an adventurer, that is trigger radical life changes. But as another celebrated contemporary of Tolkien, Andre Breton said; "transforming the world and changing your life are the same thing."[11]

Narrative does not limit itself to reflecting the world, nor to offering us a scale of values to relate to, rather it offers a vision of the world which in its encounter with history can trigger change. Tolkien writes that "every sub-creator, wishes in some measure to be a real maker, or hopes that he is drawing on reality: hopes that the peculiar quality of this secondary world (if not all the details) are derived from Reality, or are flowing into it" (OFS 77).

It is a founding principle of narration at the roots of the epic, of all epics, which always puts social values and ideas to the test, whose universality comes from the vastness and complexity of the themes and contradictions raised in the story.

And here we come to the third aspect: the thematic scope of the work. Tolkien argued that the religious element in his narrative was absorbed into the story and the symbolism (*Letters* no. 142).

---

11 Text read by Paul Eluard at the Congress of writers for the defence of literature, 21ˢᵗ June 1935, Palais de la Mutualité, Paris. Cited in Dècina Lombardi (2002:276).

Personally I am more interested in plot than symbolism. Tolkien drew from a vast wealth of stories, legends and mythologies, and even the recognizably Christian symbols take on a mythical genealogy which dates far back in time. The problem is that the symbols acquire meaning relative to the context – in other words, it is all in the eye of the beholder. We need only think of the swastika, of what it meant in human culture from the Neolithic (a symbol of good luck), versus eighty years ago in Germany, and even what it means to us today. Symbols can be made to mean many things.

This is why I favour thematic readings of texts over symbolic ones. The third part of my talk will focus on a pair of important themes in Tolkien's work: courage and power.

The finale and the end of the story; the theme of joy

Andrea Monda

On this third point perhaps Wu Ming 4 and I will not be in agreement. Even though I read in an interview a few days ago that when he read the book as a boy he was struck by the courage of the characters and the adventure, but that now he knows there to be much more in those pages – the same can certainly be said of my own experience. Over the years I have discovered many, many things residing there, hidden between the lines. George MacDonald wrote that an authentic work of art should mean many things: the truer the art, the more things it will mean (MacDonald 2000:7).

Many things, many sensations; I even remember precisely how I felt when I read it for the first time (and the second), arriving at the last page: I remember that I cried. What was the nature of those tears? Pain? Sadness? Melancholy? Joy? It is difficult to say, I think it is always difficult to define the nature of tears in men. As Borges says "you can define a polygon, but you cannot define a toothache" (Borges 1989:17-18).

Anticipating the end of my talk, I can say that I cried when faced with the beauty of those pages because "beauty hurts" (Ratzinger 2005:16) as then-cardinal Ratzinger once said, and because in that beauty I found much truth.

"Without the truth the beauty could not be" (MacDonald 2000:7), to quote MacDonald again. Father Divo Barsotti (2010) was right when he wrote that "Tolkien's story is truer than human history because at least it alerts us to a mystery which is the only truth."

At any rate, I think I had mixed feelings. Certainly those last pages (including the pages of the "Appendices" in which we find perhaps the true ending, the story of Aragorn and Arwen) pushed me not to hate the book but to love it even more, to want to understand it even more deeply. If I had to describe the sensation I felt at Frodo's departure on the last ship toward Valinor, I would say that it was one of disorientation, almost of bewilderment. Borges comes to the rescue again when he describes the essence of poetry in the feeling of those who find things "strange" (Borges 1984:28). Tolkien's ending then is a very "poetic" one. "Where are my heroes going in this strange ship?" I wondered, and to some extent I still do today (even if in the meantime I have read all of Tolkien's works and I have some idea) for the simple reason that Tolkien lets the curtain fall on the most beautiful part, gives us only a glimpse, a presentiment, of that which awaits Frodo, but he does not show it to us. In a recent conference on the rapport between poetry and mysticism in Bologna, I was invited to participate as a Tolkien expert: there I read the last page of the story, because it seems to me both "poetic" and "mystical", bringing us to the threshold that unites and divides the expressible and the inexpressible.

> "Well, here at last, dear friends, on the shores of the Sea comes the end of our fellowship in Middle-earth. Go in peace! I will not say: do not weep; for not all tears are an evil." Then Frodo kissed Merry and Pippin, and last of all Sam, and went aboard; and the sails were drawn up, and the wind blew, and slowly the ship slipped away down the long grey firth; and the light of the glass of Galadriel that Frodo bore glimmered and was lost. And the ship went out into the High Sea and passed on into the West, until at last on a night of rain Frodo smelled a sweet fragrance on the air and heard the sound of singing that came over the water. And then it seemed to him that as in his dream in the house of Bombadil, the grey rain-curtain turned all to silver glass and was rolled back, and he beheld white shores and beyond them a far green country under a swift sunrise. (*LotR* RK.VI.ix)

I would like to reflect on the ending, because in my opinion it is a crucial part of any work. It is the culmination, the summit, the moment in which the scores are settled, perhaps without hermetically sealing them but shedding a light which retrospectively illuminates the path travelled and opens it to a further dimension, that "mystery" of which Barsotti spoke and Frodo glimpses and so allows the reader a glimpse as well. One should make a careful study of story endings, of how an artist "leaves" his work, because it seems to me a distinctive moment, more intense than the rest.

As I said before, when I finished the last page of Tolkien's story, I had tears in my eyes. When I was young, the story's adventure (so naturally and marvellously told by Tolkien), the courage, the friendship, the many voices like a choir moved me... but there was already something at that time that I perceived then, and that I know now. Wu Ming 4 found complexity, philosophy; growing up I found joy in these pages. Even at the end. What is the end like: sad or joyful? Every once in a while I ask the question and it confuses. I find joy there without much difficulty. Joy permeates the novel from first to last page: from the birthday-party preparations, to the embrace between Sam and Rosie on the doorstep, from the songs which reach Frodo over the waves to Aragorn's call to Arwen not to despair; actually he says precisely: "In sorrow we must go, but not in despair. Behold! We are not bound for ever to the circles of the world, and beyond them is more than memory. Farewell!" (*LotR* App.A.I). First of all, I want to underscore the point that Wu Ming 4 made in a recent interview against the temptation to label Tolkien's work an exercise in "fogeyism" which, if this passage is any indication, is far from the truth. Even if the novel ends with the words "I'm back" (*LotR* RK.VI.ix) it has little in common with the pagan *nostoi*. Not by chance is nostalgia, in particular that of the Elves, often stigmatized by Tolkien. But let us return to Aragorn and Arwen, because one might object: but what joy is there? The two part in sadness! But the joy I am speaking of, and of which Tolkien refers to in other texts as well,[12] is Christian joy, the joy of resurrection which comes from the cross and the shadow of death. It is the joy of good which also comprises and encompasses evil. It is a full joy, this is the great promise of the Gospels, and it is indeed full, laden with all the baggage of the human experience, including the painful, transfigured by the light of hope. The joy of Tolkien's characters, I am thinking of the Hobbits as well as Gandalf (who often burst into laughter suddenly, even in the darkest moments of the story), is not

---

12 "On Fairy-stories" comes to mind as well as some passages in the letters to his children.

Boethian but full, of those who welcome the pain that joy brings with it, to use Tolkien's own expression. It is precisely the element of joy which makes it so natural for me to read this story as a story of Christian joy. Frodo, who returns to the Shire wounded, is not a John Rambo, he is not a veteran of a war who can never again find good in his country – there is much more to his character. As a boy he seemed to me the classic veteran, unable to integrate himself: the first great literary poems are essentially *nostoi*, stories of great heroes returning home. But this is not the case in *The Lord of the Rings*, at least we must not confuse Sam's role with Frodo's, which is the real lead. In addition, it is important to note that Frodo never felt completely at ease in his Shire. He, like his uncle Bilbo, has that *cor inquietum* that pushes him to leave his home. One could say that from this point of view, *The Lord of the Rings* is a book about "misfits": the Hobbits, compared to the other peoples and places of Middle-earth, do not "adapt" well and are often "out of place"; some Hobbits are not even well suited to the Shire. The entire first chapter focuses on the fact that Bilbo is viewed suspiciously by the other Hobbits, because he is bizarre, unconventional, weird. With Bilbo and Frodo we might add by association Sam, Merry and Pippin (and we would have to include the greatest misfit of all, Gollum), and these Hobbits are the protagonists of the novel, it centres on the "last (and least)" of Middle-earth, a small handful of a small people, the last of the last. The author explained it beautifully in a letter in 1963 when he said:

> We only meet exceptional hobbits in close companionship – those who had a grace or gift: a vision of beauty, and a reverence for things nobler than themselves, at war with their rustic self-satisfaction. Imagine Sam without his education by Bilbo and his fascination with things Elvish! Not difficult. The Cotton family and the Gaffer, when the "Travellers" return are a sufficient glimpse. (*Letters* no. 246)

"Exceptional" Hobbits – where the exceptionality is not within but comes from without – are "a grace or a gift". What counts is, as I explained earlier, to be ready, open, and receptive.

Frodo is a Halfling who laughs heartily, like the other Hobbits. In fact it is he who brings the power of joy into the heart of darkness on his hellish journey. At a certain point his Sam is telling him how their story might be told in the future, the story of Frodo, "the famousest of the Hobbits, and that's saying a lot":

> "It's saying a lot too much," said Frodo, and he laughed, a long clear laugh from his heart. Such a sound had not been heard in those places since Sauron came to Middle-earth. To Sam suddenly it seemed as if all the stones were listening and the tall rocks leaning over them. But Frodo did not heed them; he laughed again. "Why, Sam," he said, "to hear you somehow makes me as merry as if the story was already written. But you've left out one of the chief characters: Samwise the stouthearted. I want to hear more about Sam, dad. Why didn't they put in more of his talk, dad? That's what I like, it makes me laugh. And Frodo wouldn't have got far without Sam, would he, dad?" "Now, Mr. Frodo," said Sam, "you shouldn't make fun. I was serious." (*LotR* TT.IV.viii)

The Lord of the Rings is full of laughter like the "opening of a breach", a feeling that stays throughout the novel, for which the author coined a new word: *eucatastrophe*. Eu-catastrophe "good catastrophe" which is:

> the sudden joyous "turn" [that] does not deny the existence of *dyscatastrophe*, of sorrow and failure: the possibility of these is necessary to the joy of deliverance; it denies (in the face of much evidence, if you will) universal final defeat and in so far is *evangelium*, giving a fleeting glimpse of Joy, Joy beyond the walls of the world, poignant as grief. (OFS 75)

In the same vein, he once wrote to his son Christopher: "the sudden happy turn in a story which pierces you with a joy that brings tears" (*Letters* no. 89).

I think these are the tears I cried not only on the Field of Cormallen where we have the classic happy ending, the triumph of the small over the great, but also when we turn to the last page of the book, tears of joy. This joy is to me most important, it is what leads me to speak of Catholicism hidden between the lines of the novel, of a faith whose fundamental dimension is joy. If you had to list the essential cores of this novel, "a fundamentally religious and Catholic work", I would say there are two: joy and humility. The first is connected to the theme of the party and eucatastrophe, while the second relates to the Hobbits and their strange quest, an anti-quest where they must travel not to find and conquer but to renounce and lose. This is the heart of the novel, the other things – and there are many – are, in the end, beautiful details.

From this point of view Tolkien's novel finds itself in the centre of the 20th century, but it also represents a challenge and a response to the century which opened with Nietzsche's prophecy of the death of God but ended with the worldwide success of an English novel with Halflings at its centre. They were the only ones who could win the battle for existence, perhaps because they are small, "half", and this makes them humble, conscious of being imperfect and *monchi*, "incomplete". Tolkien's Hobbit is the *homo viator*, the pilgrim (just like Gandalf, who in addition is Grey), who knows that his life is a journey, waiting for completion in a place beyond his own strength and the confines of the world. I would like to do as Tolkien does and coin a new Italian term: Tolkien is the poet of *monchitudine*, "incompleteness", of the human condition of feeling imperfect, lacking the completion which we yearn for, and have only a presentiment of. It is no coincidence that Tolkien wanted the name of Beren inscribed on his tombstone – Beren One-hand, hero of the great love story of the First Age. Frodo, too, is maimed: Nine-fingered Frodo who returns home still deeply wounded and in search of a cure he can only find beyond the waves from where the songs come.

Baudelaire's statement about Poe comes to mind:

> The insatiable thirst for everything which lies beyond, and which life reveals, is the most living proof of our immortality. It is at the same time by poetry and through poetry, by and through music, that the soul glimpses the splendours found behind the tomb; and when an exquisite poem brings tears to one's eyes, these tears are not the sign of excessive pleasure, they are rather witness to an irritated melancholy, to a disposition of the nerves, a nature exiled among imperfect things, which would like to possess, without delay, a paradise revealed on this very same earth. (Baudelaire 2006:828)

I will conclude by saying that perhaps there is not such a great distance between me and my interlocutor. We both feel and love the richness of Tolkien's story, so full of so many things, of paganism and Catholicism. If one wanted to define the gap between us, perhaps it is in that "living proof of our immortality" which Baudelaire speaks of and which a proper work of art like Tolkien's awakens in my soul as a Catholic reader: Tolkien is not dead, he is not just a classic of the 20th century, but a friend, my friend, here, now, living. He is not a relic to be studied in a museum but a friend who walks with me, who goes before me and waits for me. Actually I feel that he is ready (like his Hobbits) and he is working hard to prepare for a party, for me – a long expected party.

The thematic scope: courage and power

Wu Ming 4

Evidently what separates my reading from Andrea Monda's is his definition of Tolkien's heroes as Christian heroes *tout court*. Obviously it would be foolish to claim that the protagonists of *The Lord of the Rings* have no connection with certain figures of the Christian tradition, especially the Hobbits, the humble, or the last destined to be first. However, Tolkien's heroes do not simply imitate such figures but belong to an intermediary category, no longer pagan but not yet Christian. In other words, they enter into a dialogue with both worlds and, accordingly, with "post-Christian" modernity as well. In order to explain myself better, I intend to speak about the philosophy of courage and the heroic model that emerge from Tolkien's pages.

The French philosopher Alain Badiou (2006) once said that "philosophy invites us to courage and also to a certain form of heroism." By courage he means the choice which lies at the root of ethics. As Professor Dumbledore of the Hogwarts School of Witchcraft and Wizardry puts it, courage is knowing how to choose between the easy way and the right way. A choice that always takes place, materially or symbolically, when humans face death (Rowling 2001:614-15; Regazzoni 2008:74-76).

In Tolkien's work we witness the contrast between two types of courage. When Frodo, after narrowly escaping from a Black Rider, realizes the danger pursuing him, he wonders: "But where shall I find courage?" (*LotR* FR.I.iii) Gildor the Elf's response is very significant: "Courage is found in unlikely places" (*LotR* FR.I.iii). It is clear that he is speaking of internal rather than geographical places. Hidden and unlikely places, not immediately apparent. That is where courage rests.

There does exist another, much more obvious courage, call it ideologized or even pathological courage. Tolkien offers us examples in all his literary works. The courage of Túrin son of Húrin, for example, is animated by the thirst for vengeance, by blind fury, and pride, from the *hybris* of feeling himself in absolute control of his destiny: Túrin *Turambar*. It is a destructive courage for the hero and everyone around him. Wrath and Pride transform Túrin from avenger to the bearer of misfortune, and they determine his tragic end, shared by Oedipus and Kullervo.

The courage of the earl Byrhtnoth in the Battle of Maldon, in the famous Anglo-Saxon poem which Tolkien studied and annotated, is also of the wrong kind. Due to his chivalrous spirit, the earl chooses death in battle, the heroic death, dragging his faithful *housecarls* with him, demonstrating a wasted and pointless nobility. Motivated by pride, Byrhtnoth chooses to defend his personal honour over his people and his country. In his famous text, "The Homecoming of Beorhtnoth Beorhthelm's Son", Tolkien suggests that the choice imposed by the Northern theory of courage is a pagan choice, even when it is made in the name of God. It is a reprehensible choice. The quest for a good death is in effect anti-Christian and there are no doubts that this hard position taken by Tolkien towards his beloved Northern heroes is due to the Christian vision of the world he shared. Like the birth of the modern, bourgeois Hobbits, it is no accident that this development emerged in the early 1930s, when a certain Germanic neo-paganism was beginning to produce monsters.

Now consider the good courage, which does not shirk even from self-sacrifice, but always in favour of the collective good. The right courage is that which Gandalf demonstrates on the Bridge of Khazad-dûm. Unlike Byrhtnoth, Gandalf holds the passage himself to guarantee the safety of the Company. It is also Frodo's when he accepts the quest to destroy the Ring. The military leaders who fight on the good side in the saga of Middle-earth never incite their men to die for the glory of a heroic ideal, but to resist until the last to save the world and their people. This is the case with Théoden at the battle of the Pelennor Fields, as it is for Bard of Esgaroth when he and his archers face the dragon Smaug.

Nevertheless, none of these heroes trusts blindly in hope (with the possible exception of Gandalf, who is, however, a messenger from the Valar, and knows something that the others do not). Actually, Tolkien's heroes are well aware that their efforts might truly be hopeless. Frodo, at a certain point, makes it explicit: "the entire adventure is without hope, so it's useless to worry about tomorrow. Probably it won't arrive" (*LotR* RK.VI.i). Later he says "no hope is left to me" (*LotR* RK.VI.ii) and he asks to borrow some from Sam, who, as we will see, succeeds in conserving it strenuously; and then later "but this is the way of the world: hope fails, the end comes" (*LotR* RK.VI.iv).

The same desperation grips Éowyn when she hopes to find death in battle, before accepting the painful, finite love of Faramir; or her brother Éomer, when he thinks that she has fallen in the field and hurls himself at his foes to the cry of "Death, death, death!" (*LotR* RK.V.vi); or Pippin when, in the last fight against Sauron's forces, he is sure that his adventure has come to an end. This is how Gandalf describes the need to challenge Sauron on the open field:

> We must walk open-eyed into that trap, with courage, but small hope for ourselves. For, my lords, it may well prove that we ourselves shall perish utterly in a black battle far from the living lands; so that even if Barad-dûr be thrown down, we shall not live to see a new age. But this, I deem, is our duty. And better so than to perish nonetheless – as we surely shall, if we sit here – and know as we die that no new age shall be. (*LotR* RK.V.ix)

Tolkien's heroes do not fight out of a spirit of testimony or with the promise of eventual recompense in the afterlife – nor could it be otherwise, given that the mythic past invented by Tolkien has not seen any Advent. In this they are "virtuous pagans" and not yet Christians. And like virtuous pagans they choose the right way over the easy way, without promise or certainty of external help (or salvation) from beyond "the circles of the world" (*LotR* App.A.I), finding in themselves the strength to resist despair.

Tom Shippey writes:

> [Frodo] has to do so furthermore by destroying the Ring, which is merely secular power and ambition, and he does so with no certain faith in rescue (or salvation) from outside, from beyond 'the circles of the world'. In this he is once again a highly contemporary figure, an image suitable for a society which as Tolkien knew perfectly well had largely lost religious faith and had no developed theory to put in its place. (Shippey 2001:187)

Tolkien's heroes are real contemporary ones because they are universal secular figures, able to speak to non-Christians and non-believers, sanctioning the wide success of the story.

The Hobbit version of courage deserves special attention. In *The Hobbit*, when Bilbo decides to betray his companions to avert the imminent war by handing over the Arkenstone to the other side, he makes a gesture which enables others to start diplomatic negotiations, though it brings down the curses of Thorin and the Dwarves on Bilbo's head. It is a sort of righteous betrayal which definitely requires the right kind of courage.

It is the kind of courage that Bilbo demonstrates numerous times throughout *The Hobbit*, getting the better part of his nostalgia for home, laziness, and hesitance. This part is not simply baggage though; it is an important component of Hobbit heroism. Just as his "adventurous" side pushes him to leave home and transform his life, this "domestic" side helps to balance and keep in check the heroic impulse, preventing heroism from becoming an end in itself, an aesthetic or ideological act like Byrhtnoth's.

This is a peculiar characteristic of Hobbits and the type of heroism they embody, as even Thorin Oakenshield understands at his death, when he says that "some courage and some wisdom, blended in measure" (*H* XVIII) are found in Bilbo.

The courage or heroism of Hobbits is in fact composite. It is not only blended with wisdom, but also qualified by two fundamental elements.

The first is a sense of humour, which Hobbits can rely on even in the most difficult situations, and which is an excellent antidote to pride. Finding a comic side to even the worst predicament, Hobbits continuously reaffirm their limits, their being out of place. Only by relying on this paradox are they able to carry out the task. It is clear that self-irony does not stop them from sacrifice in the service of the collective good: even though they are not ascetic warriors, but lovers of simple pleasures and earthly joys, Hobbits are neither cynical nor egotistical. Their amused laughter is not the contemptuous sneer of the warrior who throws himself toward death, nor the sardonic smile of one who contemplates his own and others' fates with detachment, but an homage to life, able to resonate loudly even in the desolation of Mordor.

However, their sense of humour does not coincide with Christian joy, which, as Andrea Monda reminds us, passes through the cross and the shadow of death and which at all times looks to the promise of an otherworldly dimension able to amend human imperfection. On the contrary, it is an attitude generated by a connection with the concreteness and materiality of earthly life. This is demonstrated in an even more meaningful manner by the second element in Hobbit heroism, which we have already seen in Bilbo, and which keeps hope alive for Sam: the memory of the good life.

When Sam believes that Frodo is dead, lost in the land of Mordor, he sits dejectedly and begins to remember all he has left behind. He murmurs "old childish tunes of the Shire" (*LotR* RK.VI.i) and songs which evoke "fleeting glimpses of the country of his home" (*LotR* RK.VI.i); he remembers summer baths, the beautiful Rosie Cotton basking in sunlight; the taste of food. The more the chance of returning from the quest alive dwindles, the more his thoughts turn to the pleasant things he has left behind. It is not the prospective of an afterlife that gives him hope, but the memory of the good things enjoyed in this life.

All this does no good for Frodo who, under the weight of the Ring, is incapable of remembering anything: "No taste of food, no feel of water, no sound of wind, no memory of tree or grass or flower, no image of moon or star are left to me" (*LotR* RK.VI.iii).

This lapse of memory signals his defeat. At the last step Frodo gives in to the temptation of Power and claims the Ring for himself. Even though just moments later the Ring is providentially taken by Gollum and destroyed as he falls into the abyss, Frodo understands that once the border into the Shadow is crossed he can no longer make a full return to himself: "There is no real going back. Though I may come to the Shire, it will not seem the same; for I shall not be the same. [...] Where shall I find rest?" (*LotR* RK.VI.vii).

The answer arrives at the end of the story, when he is granted the priviledge of sailing to the blessed realm of Valinor where he may find the peace he needs.

Now, even if we were to follow Andrea Monda in his reading of Frodo's voyage to Valinor as a clear reference to the salvation beyond the world in form of the Christian Heaven, thus applying the strict allegorical reading Tolkien so disliked, the fact remains that we know nothing of Frodo's destiny in the land of the Valar. In fact, Tolkien, by refusing to push the narration beyond the borders of our world, assumes an attitude that stands in stark contrast to Dante. And though it is also true that he tells us that "beyond them is more than memory" (*LotR* App.A.I), he is nevertheless careful not to reveal what this further dimension consists of. We have only a fleeting glimpse of Valinor, caught through Frodo's eyes from the deck of the last ship, on the last page of *The Lord of the Rings*. This suspension of the story, echoed at the end of "Leaf by Niggle", confirms once again that Tolkien's heroism is independent from happy endings or the faith we cultivate in the unknowable fate that awaits us after death.

Lastly, there is another fundamental quality found in Hobbits that I would like to discuss. It is a quality that we encounter in all the positive figures of Tolkien's stories, i.e. their total lack of interest in honour and honours, let alone power. There is no heroic ideal which predetermines their moves and they have no desire to dominate others. This is made blatantly clear when Sam finds himself carrying the Ring. For him the temptation takes the form of becoming "Samwise the Strong, Hero of the Age" (*LotR* RK.VI.i). His response is to re-establish his priorities; anything beyond this would be *hybris*: "The one small garden of a free gardener was all his need and due, not a garden swollen to a realm; his own hands to use, not the hands of others to command" (*LotR* RK.VI.i).

This is the point: in Tolkien's narrative courage is contrasted with power (it is not by chance that "Power" is most frequently used in connection with Sauron). As I was saying, this is not only true for small Hobbits but for their big companions, too. Gandalf and Aragorn, in particular, always look to convince others, not to force them. Since power is coercive, it is an exercise in domination, something that Tolkien's heroes always refuse, not only in dealing with friends but also with enemies. Everyone is given a choice, even the traitor Saruman.

The courage of Tolkien's heroes is to refuse power while at the same time to accept the responsibility to act for the common good. This attitude (or ethos) stands in opposition to the desire for power in order to achieve things in the collective interest, which is the typical attitude of the politician, be s/he conservative, reformist, or revolutionary. It is this paradoxical affirmation found in Tolkien's narrative that re-establishes one of the central qualities of Christianity and, at the same time, thwarts the potential anti-worldly drift by linking it to the need to confront evil in history. Tolkien's heroes do not resign themselves to the unfolding of iniquity and to act out the dialectic of light vs. shadow within themselves. Sauron's tyranny must be opposed by Aragorn's regality. Aragorn who, unlike Thorin in *The Hobbit*, uses the weight of his lineage with extreme caution, taking up his reign only *after* Sauron is defeated since he is aware that staking his claim before that could easily cause internal disagreements among the Free Peoples. And again: after becoming king by consensus and not by imposition, he offers freedom and peace to all the peoples of Middle-earth, including those who fought for Sauron.

Tolkien himself, in his private writings, makes explicit his belief that man was not born to command his neighbour and affirms that "the most improper job of any man, even saints (who at any rate were at least unwilling to take it on), is bossing other men" (*Letters* no. 52).

The desire to dominate things, to assert yourself over others, even for the best of intentions, is the beginning of corruption and sets off a chain of adverse events. It is irrelevant whether this is done to raise your artistic skills to new heights, like Fëanor in ancient times, or to protect your own people, as Boromir desires. Such an attitude corrupts you by accepting the belief that the ends justify the means and that the Machine can be used in our strive for the common good. But the Ring of Power cannot be used to any good ends, it can only produce more power that is in itself subservient to it. The only way to defeat evil is to destroy the means of its perpetuation.

So if means and ends coincide (or strategy and tactics coincide, as T.E. Lawrence would say), then who we are and what we do are one and the same. It follows that there is nothing more political and ethical in our very existence, each one of us carries a moral instance strictly tied to practical action. It is not possible to count oneself out and say "I have nothing to do with it", believing we can avoid the conflict. As Gandalf's words to Frodo remind us: "and you must therefore use such strength and heart and wits as you have" (*LotR* FR.I.ii).

I would like to conclude by saying that the theme of power is undoubtedly connected to that of death and immortality, identified by Tolkien as the key theme of *The Lord of the Rings*. Power in fact does not accept the idea of death, it must presume itself to be infinite and eternal. Power never passes the baton, it can only be overturned or destroyed or, in fact, defeated by death. It is no coincidence that great men of power in history have rarely understood how to create the necessary conditions for a peaceful handover. The death of a great leader is usually followed by a power vacuum and a battle without quarter between subordinates. Because even when it purports to lay claim to a paternal role, power is more easily master than father. And this is the clearest demonstration of its sterility.

About the Authors

ANDREA MONDA obtained a degree in Religious Science at the Pontifical Gregorian University. His thesis on theological meanings of *The Lord of the Rings* has been published by Rubbettino Editore under the title *L'Anello e la Croce* in 2008. He works as a teacher of the Catholic religion in the high schools of Rome, the Pontifical Gregorian University, and the Pontifical Lateran University. He has furthermore published, together with Saverio Simonelli, *Tolkien, il Signore della Fantasia* (Frassinelli, 2002) and *Gli Anelli della Fantasia* (Frassinelli, 2004), with Paolo Gulisano *Il Mondo di Narnia* (SanPaolo 2005) and with Giovanni Cucci *L'Arazzo rovesciato. L'Enigma del Male* (Cittadella Editrice, 2010).

WU MING 4 is a member of Wu Ming ("No Name" in Chinese), a collective of writers that wrote several novels translated in many countries, such *Q*, *54*, *Manituana* and *Altai*. Wu Ming also run *Giap*, one of the most important political and cultural blogs in Italy: (www.wumingfoundation.com/giap), on whose pages Wu Ming 4 developed his reading of Tolkien's works in accordance with the most important interpretations in the anglophone world. J.R.R. Tolkien is one of the main characters of Wu Ming 4's solo novel *Stella del Mattino* (Einaudi, 2008). WM4 also edited the new Italian edition of Tolkien's *The Homecoming of Beorhtnoth Beorhthelm's Son* (Bompiani, 2010), and is the author of *Difendere la Terra di Mezzo: scritti su J.R.R.Tolkien* (Odoya, 2013). During the years 2010-12, he held seminars at the University of Pesaro and Urbino, as part of the course "Teoria e pratiche della narrazione".

Bibliography

BADIOU, Alain. 2006. "Il coraggio della felicità." Interview available on http://d.repubblica.it/dmemory/2006/01/28/attualita/attualita/118sar484118.html.

BARSOTTI, Divo. 2010. "Appendice." In Joseph PEARCE. 2010. *Tolkien: l'uomo e il mito*. Genova-Milano: Marietti.

BAUDELAIRE, Charles. 2006. *Opere*. Milano: Mondadori.

BORGES, Jorge L. 1984. *Conversazioni americane*. Roma: Editori Riuniti.

——. 1989. *Altre conversazioni*. Milano: Bompiani.

——. 1990. *Ultime conversazioni*. Milano: Bompiani.

CARVER, Raymond. 2002. *Per favore non facciamo gli eroi. Saggi, poesie, racconti*. Roma: Minimum Fax.

CHESTERTON, Gibert K. 1980. *Ortodossia*. Brescia: Morcelliana.

——. 2008. *L'uomo eterno*. Soveria Mannelli: Rubbettino.

DÈCINA LOMBARDI, Paola. 2002. *Surrealismo 1919-1969. Ribellione e immaginaizione*. Roma: Editori Riuniti.

DELEUZE, Gilles and Félix GUATTARI. 1996. *Che cos'è la filosofia?* Torino: Einaudi.

DUPONT, Jacques. 1992. *Le Beatitudini*. Cinisello Balsamo, Edizioni Paoline.

GRAVES, Robert. 1992. *La Dea Bianca*. Milano: Adelphi.

GREEN, Graham. 1958. "Perché scrivo." In *Saggi cattolici*. Milano, Mondadori, 139-159.

GROTTA, Daniel. 1983. *Vita di J.R.R. Tolkien*. Milano: Rusconi.

MACDONALD, George. 2000. *La favola del giorno e della notte*. Milano: Mondadori.

MONDA, Andrea. 2008. *L'Anello e la Croce*. Soveria Mannelli: Rubbettino.

O'CONNOR, Flannery. 1993. *Nei territori del diavolo*. Roma: Theoria.

——. 2001. *Sola a presidiare la fortezza*. Torino: Einaudi.

PAREYSON, Luigi. 1987. "I problemi attuali dell'estetica." In *Momenti e problemi di Storia dell'Estetica*. Milano: Marzorati, 1805-1967.

PASTERNAK, Boris. 1960. *Il Dottor Živago*, Milano: Feltrinelli.

RAHNER, Karl. 1964. "La biblioteca parrocchiale. Principi per una teologia del libro." In *Missione e Grazia. Saggi di teologia pastorale*. Roma: Edizioni Paoline, 693-725.

RATZINGER, Joseph. 2005. *La bellezza. La Chiesa*. Roma: Itaca.

REGAZZONI, Simone. 2008. *Harry Potter e la filosofia*. Genova: Il Melangolo.

ROWLING, Joanne K. 2001. *Harry Potter e il Calice di Fuoco*. Milano: Salani.

SALVARANI, Brunetto. 2004. *In principio era il racconto*. Bologna: EMI.

SHIPPEY, Tom A. 2001. *J.R.R. Tolkien. Author of the Century*. London: HarperCollins.

SIMONELLI, Saverio. 2000. "I cattolici fuori dalle antologie." *Avvenire*, 2 February 2000.

SPADARO, Antonio. 2009. *Alla ricerca del lupo*. Bologna: Pardes.

TOLKIEN, John and Priscilla TOLKIEN. 1992. *The Tolkien Family Album*. Wilmington MA: Houghton Mifflin Company.

VON BALTASHAR, Hans Urs. 1978. *Stili ecclesiali*. Milano: Jaca Book.

1983. *La semplicità del cristiano*. Milano: Jaca Book.

WU MING 4. 2010a. *L'eroe imperfetto*, Milano: Bompiani.

2010b. "Prefazione." In *Il ritorno di Beorhtnoth figlio di Beorhthelm*. Milano: Bompiani.

Works by J.R.R. Tolkien

H: *The Hobbit: or, There and Back Again*, ed. Douglas A. Anderson, London: HarperCollins, 2001.

Letters: *The Letters of J.R.R. Tolkien*, ed. Humphrey Carpenter and Christopher Tolkien, London: HarperCollins, 1999.

LotR: *The Lord of the Rings*, 50th anniversary edition, Boston: Houghton Mifflin, 2004.

OFS: "On Fairy-Stories", first published in *Essays Presented to Charles William*, London: Oxford University Press, 1947, pp. 38-89, reprinted in *TL*.

TL: *Tree and Leaf*, London: HarperCollins, 2001.

Christopher Garbowski

Tolkien's Philosophy and Theology of Death

I have been asked to write about Tolkien's philosophy and theology of death. Since by his own admission death is a major theme in the author's best known work, *The Lord of the Rings*, it is only natural to discuss what can be called his philosophy of death. However, although for scholars aware of the vast literature on religious readings of Tolkien, not to mention readers of *The Silmarillion*, the topic may seem at least familiar, for many ordinary readers a "theology" of death requires some explanation.

Moreover, theological readings among scholars are likewise not uncontroversial. It is well known that Tolkien himself was a practising Catholic. By no means wishing to impose his views on others and stressing the freedom of the reader, in *The Lord of the Rings*, he nevertheless created a narrative that for the perceptive reader points beyond itself. Part of this is due to the intentional strategy on Tolkien's part to remove all religious cults and practices from the work so that, as he put it, "the religious element is absorbed into the story and the symbolism" (*Letters* no. 142). Some critics have accepted this explanation and speak of the author as, among others, "sanctifying myth". Others question the author and consider the work to contain, alongside theistic, substantial "pagan" elements.[1] As Fleming Rutledge puts it in more general terms, "The Rings saga contains a powerful undercurrent of transcendent meaning. This undercurrent can be interpreted in varying ways, not all of these will be theological" (Rutledge 2004:8).

Many authors point to a number of religious commentaries that Tolkien himself volunteered about his work in his published correspondence. This makes it easier to deal with a subject like the one I will discuss. Yet these are not the only opinions he has given. For instance, during an interview for BBC he favorably quoted a passage from Simone de Beauvoir where she claims that death is an

---

1 See Hutton (2008:39).

"unjustifiable violation" for everyone.² Such a sentiment is even present in the post-*Rings* tale "Athrabeth Finrod ah Andreth", a story chronologically set in the First Age of Middle-earth. In it the theme of death figures largely in the dialogue between Finrod and Athrabeth. When the High Elf Finrod hints at the special status of humans, the wise woman Athrabeth reiterates the different experience of death among Men and Elves, concluding that the fate of people means that "dying we die, and we go out to no return. Death is an uttermost end, a loss irremediable" (*Morgoth* 311).

Nonetheless, bearing in mind that theological interpretations are not the only ones on the topic, whether it is considered seminal or partial, my focus will primarily be from that perspective. Moreover, I feel it should be taken into account that Tolkien's theology of death is inseparable from his theology of life with its *telos*. And both are better placed in the context of his theology of narrative, as he theorized it and as it emerges in his work. In other words, I will attempt to examine his theology and philosophy of death, which are largely interchangeable for me, within their broadest possible context in his thought and work.

Starting with Tolkien as a theologian, while it may be true that the author did not have a formal training in theology, which at times shows in some of the opinions he proffers, a number of scholars nonetheless attribute profound theological intuition to some of his ideas and also find it implicit in his creative work.³ The simplest definition of theology is "faith seeking understanding", which to some degree makes everyone who wishes to integrate his or her faith more fully within his or her life a theologian.

Tolkien himself claimed that "our ideas about God and ways of expressing them will be largely derived from contemplating the world about us" (*Letters* no. 310). This world can be considered both the larger world around us and our own private world. At this juncture I'd like to point out that rather meager attention has been given to the influence of his family life on his theology, or even creativity. Tolkien himself broached the latter topic in the allegorical short story "Leaf by Niggle". In it he splits his social-familial and creative sides into

---

2 I am citing de Beauvoir after Armstrong (1998:10-12).
3 Alison Milbank is among the latest and most perceptive scholars to analyze Tolkien the theologian. See Milbank 2009.

two characters, Parish and Niggle, and shows how at one level they conflict with each other, but at a transcendent one Niggle's art benefits from Parish's constant "interference".

But family and society is not just duties: as the father of four children it also meant participation in "creation". Substantial evidence points to the impact of fertility on religious observance in societies. Social scientist Mary Eberstadt asks the question why this relationship holds, suggesting, among others:

> there is the phenomenological fact of what birth does to many fathers and just about every mother. That moment [...] is routinely experienced by a great many people as an event transcendental as no other. [...] The sequence of events culminating in birth is nearly universally interpreted as a moment of communion with something larger than oneself, larger even than oneself and the infant.[4]

In a letter Tolkien himself describes the intense effect that the birth of his son Christopher had on him: "you were so special a gift to me, in a time of sorrow and mental suffering, and your love, opening at once almost as soon as you were born, that I am consoled ever by the certainty that there is no end to this" (*Letters* no. 64). There is some evidence that, unlike from the 1930s on, for a number of years after WWI Tolkien's faith was lukewarm, and that this state was largely overcome while his family grew says something of the possible impact of parenthood and family life on his understanding and experiencing of his faith.

In my opinion it is in this imponderable sphere that we possibly should look for the roots to an unusual fact concerning an author who was both an orphan and a witness of the carnage of total war, both of which influenced his strongly pessimistic personal bent (Carpenter 2002:50 *passim*). Namely, if death is quite understandably a major implicit theme in *The Lord of the Rings*, it must also be remembered that Tolkien's theology of narrative art is essentially comedic. This constitutes a particularly striking tension in the work: one might say it is better resolved on the theological than philosophical level, but even the theology is far from predictable.

Before I explore this it is worth examining what might arguably be called one of the deeper sources of the author's theology. Among others, it is important to

---

4 Elberstadt (2007:12-13).

consider the dynamics of what has been termed the religious imagination and how it affects theological perception, even in people without formal theological training. According to the theologian David Tracy, the theistic imagination is on the one hand dialectical, picturing God as distant from creation, on the other hand it is analogical, wherein God is also felt to be close to the world and to people (Greeley 2000:5-9). Although the relationship of these two tendencies is dynamic and shifting, the Catholic imagination inclines toward accepting the closeness of God to creation. This, among others, is the reason for the importance of the sacraments, which give evidence of the availability of grace to God's creatures. The religious sensibility that evolves from this perspective is adept at perceiving metaphors that demonstrate the proximity of God to humanity, and values human community. In contrast, the dialectical tendency, for which the Protestant sensibility has a greater affinity, tends to view community as an obstacle to a more direct relationship with God. Andrew Greeley summarizes the different sensibilities: "Catholics tend to accentuate the immanence of God, Protestants the transcendence of God" (Greeley 2000:5). Tracy stresses the complementarity of the two religious sensibilities and that neither is superior to the other, while Greeley, a sociologist, has studied how they become embodied in the art, literature and attitudes of society, particularly in the United States. He demonstrates that there is a connection between the religious imagination and how people live and also the themes that permeate their creativity.

Tolkien's claim cited above of making inferences about God from studying the world is certainly in line with his religious heritage and its attendant sensibility. Earlier I have written about the predominance of the analogical (i.e. Catholic) imagination in Tolkien's work.[5] To some extent this claim corresponds with Ralph Wood's sweeping analysis of the contrast between Tolkien and his fellow Inkling, C.S. Lewis:

> For Lewis it is possible for the Gospel to exist without the ethos which it creates. Thus did he discern a potential divide between Christ and culture that Tolkien never observed. Whereas Tolkien sought to build up what might be called a Christian culture, Lewis was an evangelist who sought first and last to make the case for Christianity, whether by straightforward argument [...] or by fictional embodiment [...]. (Wood 2003b:318)

---

5 See Garbowski (2003:9-12).

However, a personal theology does not have to be fully consistent. When one considers, for instance, that the texts that Tolkien the scholar studied most closely, i.e. those of the Old and Middle English periods, were written before the Reformation, and thus to some degree combined both theistic sensibilities, then we can see at least a possible source of the theological complexity in his views regarding contrasting religious sensibilities.[6]

However, although in his *Beowulf* essay Tolkien famously admires virtues of Northern courage, I would largely agree with Wood that "he could not finally affirm the overwhelming darkness and hopelessness of [its] outlook" (Wood 2003a:75). In his essay "On Fairy-stories", he develops a comedic narrative theology. Comedy understood in contradistinction to tragedy is based on the ethical value of happiness. Happiness, or human flourishing, was understood as a primary ethical goal by most ancient moral philosophers in the Occident as well as being accepted by Christianity. One scholar notes that for Christian thinkers like Aquinas, "happiness is a process, a continual becoming, in which we realize our full potential by fully realizing ourselves" (McMahon 2006:132). Moreover, human flourishing was intended to go beyond personal excellence and contribute to strengthening the sense of community.

Returning to Tolkien's essay: much as happiness is the proper end of the virtuous life, joy is the proper end of the fairy tale, or fantasy. Tolkien takes this "joyous turn", or "eucatastrophe", as he famously termed it, of the fairy story, to a theological *climax* by claiming that it gains its strength through faintly echoing the Gospel story, while the Gospel story in turn absorbs fairy stories by fulfilling the desires embodied in them in the real world. Verlyn Flieger points out that for Tolkien the fairy story becomes a kind of conversion experience, taking the reader from despair to joy (Flieger 2002:31).

It should be pointed out, however, that for Tolkien sub-creation is not in any way a supernatural process. "The main trajectory of faerie mediation", suggests Alison Milbank, "is towards this world, and towards its redemption from our greedy appropriation" (Milbank 2009:168). Sub-creation is a religious activity, we might say "concurring in God's work", but not a religion in itself. That is

---

6 Tom Shippey, for one, looks at some of the differing theological views in early English literature and its relation to Catholic doctrine. See Shippey (2005:175-81).

a necessary distinction in regards to the modernist view that with advancing secularization art replaces religion. As David Morgan (2008:40) puts it:

> Moving throughout the discourse of Modernism in art was a dominant conception of the sacred, one which distanced art from institutional religion, most importantly Christianity, in order to secure the freedom of art as an autonomous cultural force that was sacralized in its own right.

That Tolkien was concerned with the processes of secularization and its effects seems to be indicated in his relating sub-creation to the "craft" of "enchantment" (*MC* 143). Enchantment as a critical term stands in contradistinction to Max Weber's "disenchantment". But in Tolkien's case it is not so simple. As Charles Taylor explains it, disenchantment is, among others, the sense which came into existence with the development of science that "there is absolutely no question of higher meanings being *expressed* in the universe around us", while, traditionally, in an enchanted world "there is a strong contrast between the sacred and the profane" (Taylor 2007:446). Nevertheless, although it may be true that in his fiction Tolkien's "enchantment" may look anachronistic, i.e. depicting a world with the presence of spirits and demons etc., the concept in the essay is not a mere return to an irretrievable past. It should be noted that his idea of "re-enchantment" strongly critiques a particular byproduct of disenchantment, i.e. "the active instrumental stance toward the world" (Taylor 2007:98), which he terms "magic". "Magic produces or pretends to produce", claims Tolkien, "an alteration in the Primary World. It does not matter by whom it is said to be practiced, fay or mortal, it remains distinct from [enchantment]; it is not an art but a technique; its desire is *power* in this world, domination of things and wills" (*MC* 143).[7] Tolkien is not against science as such, which in its pure form represents "the spirit that desires knowledge of other things, their history and nature, *because they are 'other'* and wholly independent of the enquiring mind" (*Letters* no. 153). Enchantment as art is superior to "magic" in that it can create a Secondary World without in any way disrupting or dominating the Primary World, and this is true Art.

The means of achieving true art is sub-creation. I might add that if "true Art" and "sub-creation" sounds quite lofty, in practice it was not necessarily so. It is significant that one of the early critics of *The Lord of the Rings*, who Tolkien

---

7 See also Curry 1999 and Bachmann 2007.

felt captured something of the creative process, noted that his novel constituted "an elaborate form of *game* of inventing a country" (*Letters* no. 154). It is quite interesting to note the similarities between Tolkien's concept of sub-creation and Johan Huizinga's concept of play elaborated in his *Homo Ludens*. For instance Tolkien insisted on the seriousness of the sub-created world, since irony would destroy it. Huizinga talks about the importance of rules in play, since as soon as rules are transgressed "the whole play-world collapses" (Huizinga 2002:11). Huizinga even writes of the end of the game as the end of the spell, relating play to enchantment. On their own terms and levels, sub-creation and play create worlds. What is significant here is not only that a scholar of philology and a scholar of cultural history come up with similar concepts not too many years apart during the late thirties, but that they both were deeply interested in and fascinated by the culture and art of the Middle Ages – a culture strongly influenced by Aquinas's conception of beauty as that which delights. If the scholars were not influenced by Aquinas directly, it might have been the culture that inspired them, as indeed it might have inspired the concept in the scholastic thinker.

Huizinga's concept of play has been termed "ludology", and, of course, has returned to inspire scholars in the study of video games. Again one might point out the coincidence that Tolkien's Middle-earth was one of the sources of inspiration for role-playing games such as *Dungeons and Dragons*. This might be related to the fact that beauty that delights, among other things, by giving an imaginary world structure and following specific rules, inspires participation.

The above discussion is hardly complete, but it gives a rudimentary idea of the conceptual and theological notions that to no small degree Tolkien eventually incorporated in his creative production. Nonetheless, during the course of his creative, or sub-creative work the concepts gained a number of nuances and a variety of problems and issues were explored.

As is well-known, Tolkien's earliest and ultimately unfinished creative work is the mythopoeic Middle-earth *legendarium* from which his son Christopher posthumously fashioned *The Silmarillion*, and which was eventually chronicled in the twelve volumes of the *History of Middle-earth*. In a letter to an early reader of *The Lord of the Rings* Tolkien referred to the opus as "from beginning to end [...] mainly concerned with the relation of Creation to making and sub-creation", adding parenthetically: "and subsidiarily with the related matter of 'mortality'" (*Letters* no. 153). We will return to the latter later, but clearly he links his creative work with his theology of narrative from "On Fairy-stories". The mythology contains a creation story, which is a thinly veiled hymn of praise of the "Creation" of the Primary World: "And this habitation might seem a little thing to those who consider only [...] the immeasurable vastness of the World which still the Ainur are shaping, and not the minute precision to which they shape all things therein" (*S Ainul*). In its relation to "Creation", the splendor of the Middle-earth cosmos offers an invitation to examine it at many levels, thus approximating an Aristotelian metaphysics. As Wood (2003b:325) puts it, for Tolkien "transcendent reality is to be found in the depths of this world rather than in some putative existence beyond it."

As an enchanted world Middle-earth evokes wonder in the reader. Even the grotesque works in tandem with this purpose. As Milbank (2009:67) puts it, "the monsters of Tolkien's art are facts of Middle-earth life that the reader does not fully comprehend; and in so acting they dramatize the unknowability of its universe." Nonetheless, one of the striking things about Tolkien's sub-created world and likewise pertinent to our discussion is its ordered nature.[8] The Catholic imagination recognizes the need for hierarchy for a healthy community or, as Greeley puts it, the necessity of structure: "Structure implies organization, which is not possible without leadership, which in turn requires hierarchy. [...] Hierarchy is implicit in the notion of community because without leadership community soon descends into anarchy" (Greeley 2000:138).[9] Wood argues that the hierarchical structure of Middle-earth is grounded in the author's religious sensibility (Wood 2003a:38). The wish to provide readers with a hierarchically structured world therefore demonstrates that the desire for order is part of the motivation behind his sub-created world. And so we have a hierarchy from inanimate and animate beings, to sentient beings of which humans are not even on the top, on up to Ilúvatar the godhead. One might add that this hierarchy

---

8 See e.g. Zimbardo (2004:68-75).
9 While it is true Tolkien called himself politically an "anarchist," in his creative work it is more correct to say he was searching for a model of proper leadership.

largely complies with the Catholic principle of subsidiarity in that the benign sentient creatures are generally aware of the limits of their competence.

Thus in the unfolding narrative of Tolkien's mythology there is a dialogic cosmology in which Ilúvatar is aided by angelic beings, or Valar. Some of the immortal Elves have met these incorporated angelic beings and live long enough to relate their meetings to Men. However, by the Third Age, the period when *The Lord of the Rings* is set, most of these select Elves have either died in the numerous battles or left Middle-earth. And so the continuing action of Ilúvatar in Middle-earth largely resembles that of God's in our own world. Providence is implied and even recognized at a number of junctures, such as when Gandalf suggests that Frodo was "meant" to find the Ring. However, its subtlety and the fact that often providence can only be detected in hindsight, has moral and dramatic significance in the narrative. As Thomas Hibbs (2003:170) puts it, "[t|he mysterious, incomprehensible designs of providence underscore the importance of human effort, a sense that, in spite of the apparent odds, one must press on to do one's duty in the fight against evil."

Within the ordered world of *The Lord of the Rings*, the presence of community is an essential prerequisite for a fulfilled human existence. Such an emphasis is quite close to the Catholic imagination. Greeley (2000:130) suggests that "under ordinary conditions Catholics picture society as supportive and not oppressive." Hibbs (2003:173) points out that "Tolkien gives us characters who can only understand themselves as parts of larger wholes, as members of nations and races, as participants in alliances and friendships for the good, and ultimately as part of a natural cosmos."

Tolkien initially establishes the theme of community in the novel by presenting the Hobbits and their ways. These fundamentally simple people are full of *joie de vivre*. If, as Greeley (2000:52) says, the Catholic imagination loves festivals and leisure and that it "revels in stories that are festivals and festivals that are stories", then the presence of the Hobbits and all they represent are the primary manifestation of this Catholic sensibility in *The Lord of the Rings*. It is interesting to note that Tolkien's Protestant friend C.S. Lewis was somewhat irritated by the Hobbits, and felt that Tolkien overdid their presence in the work.[10] The analogical and dialectical imaginations affect not only the creative process, but to some extent also the reception of a work of art.

Beneath their flair for the festive, and closely related to it, is the Hobbits' propensity to form friendships. Not only classical philosophers such as Aristotle, but also today's positive psychologists stress the importance of friendship for happiness – an idea which can be related to the moral economy of eudaimonism in *The Lord of the Rings*. The Hobbits also represent the economy of self-transcendence present in the novel. They seem at times childlike to the reader and to those they encounter. But they grow through the gift of themselves. As Milbank (2009:140) comments on Sam and Frodo's less noted friends, "it is by giving themselves that the Hobbits grow and develop, both physically and morally and from 'flotsam and jetsam' to full personhood as Peregrin and Meriadoc."

Yet, if the workings of providence are quite subtle in Middle-earth, the forces of evil are blatantly overt. Despite Tolkien's claim that the theme of domination is not the most important one in *The Lord of the Rings*, there is no denying the persuasive narrative of the struggle against evil and domination in the novel. Tom Shippey, among others, has detected a Manichean strain in the presentation of evil in the work, but a number of scholars tend to see Tolkien's "enchanted" conception of evil as largely Augustinian in that it is essentially parasitical on goodness. In *The Lord of the Rings* this is most explicit when Elrond says: "For nothing is evil in the beginning. Even Sauron was not so" (*LotR* FR.II.ii). That Frodo, one of the heroes of the novel, succumbs to the power of the Ring, is consistent with Tolkien's often expressed conviction that "the power of evil is too great to be resisted by incarnate creatures without divine aid" (Rutledge 2004:10). This is also a factor that makes *The Lord of the Rings* not simply a binary "good versus evil" tale: the best characters either realize that evil is not only in the "other", but also a potential within themselves, or they learn this at some point in the narrative. Indeed, bar-

---

10 In a similar manner Fleming Rutledge, who also proffers a Protestant Reading of *The Lord of the Rings*, is fairly dismissive of its introductory chapters that focus on the Hobbits' lifestyle.

ring the *climax*, the evil Ring is most of the time in the hands of the "good" characters for the duration of the novel.

Tolkien counters evil in *The Lord of the Rings*, or the "Shadow", with light, i.e. the "primary and independent" goods that justify and support the comedic structure of Middle-earth. An opposition to the parasitic nature of evil would be the noted "diversity of good" contrasting with "the sameness of evil" (Rosebury 2003:42) permeating the work. In the narrative economy of *The Lord of the Rings* it is the benign richness of Middle-earth that makes the struggle against evil all the more vivid. Dramatically this functions by producing the effect that

> the reader must be delighted in Middle-earth in order to care that Sauron does not lay it desolate, and must endorse with a lively emotional response the claims of the Shire, Rivendell, Lothlórien and Gondor, of Gandalf, Aragorn and Frodo, to constitute images of a life that is to be desired in oneself and others. (Rosebury 2003:41)

Effectively, the sub-created world's benign richness supports the comedic structure of the narrative that validates the eucatastrophe of its closure.

One critic further frames the contrast as that between the possessive and imitative desire of evil, which ultimately has no substance, and the authentic being of goodness, which has no desire for possession.[11] Authentic being is shared to a greater or lesser extent in Middle-earth by its benign peoples. These peoples are all fallible, but the good characters are guided by human virtues that are completed by grace: "Tolkien the Christian imbues *The Lord of the Rings* not only with pagan virtues as they are classically conceived", Wood (2003a:77) argues, "but also with the conviction that, when completed and perfected, prudence issues in holy folly, justice in undeserved mercy, courage in unexpected endurance, and temperance in joyful self-denial." Joyful self-denial is a key here. Among others, the virtue provides an advantage over evil, personified by Sauron, who, for all his power and malicious intelligence, "cannot imagine selflessness" (Rutledge 2004:162), which ultimately leads to his downfall.

The greatest self-denial, however, is the acceptance of death. Tolkien claimed in his correspondence that together with immortality the theme of death is

---

11 Head (2007:147).

dominant in *The Lord of the Rings*. It pervades the novel structurally, in his own words, through "the mystery of the love of the world in the hearts of a race 'doomed' to leave and seemingly lose it [and] the anguish in the hearts of a race 'doomed' not to leave it, until the whole evil-aroused story is complete" (*Letters* no. 186). Tolkien is referring to the contrast between human beings, with their short life-spans, and Elves, who possess the potential of deathlessness. Thus the contrasting state of the latter acts as a thematic foil. As Flieger (1997:108) observes, "Elves and Men are mirrors of one another; they embody one another's deepest wishes and tell escapist stories about one another." We might recall Tolkien's claim in "On Fairy-stories" that the fairy tale expresses the deep human desire of "the Escape from Death" (*MC* 153).

Tolkien's Middle-earth also contains various undead, such as the Ringwraiths,[12] which, while originally conceived, have their correlates in popular culture, such as zombies or vampires. In Tolkien's version there is an element of the Aristotelian sense that only natural existence is a good thing. As philosopher Bill Davis (2003:126) puts it: "When any natural thing is prevented from fulfilling its natural purpose, it is frustrated. [...] Similarly, for the Ringwraiths, unending existence is a fate worse than death; it involves the perpetual pain of having their natures frustrated."

The Elves, however, are a positive example of "immortality", or at least seemingly so. While Elves are "naturally" deathless, their life-span is connected to the duration of life on earth and they are not known to be included in the Second Music of the Ainur at the end of time as Men are. At this point I must interject that the Second Music of the Ainur is one of the more interesting elements in Tolkien's artistic vision of the afterlife, especially in light of a number of contemporary philosophical discussions regarding the alleged monotony of heaven (Davis 2003:132-33). Tolkien's dynamic vision of plenitude in the form of humanity's ultimate destiny as sub-creators obviously does not constitute an argument, or if it does, one more of a theological nature, but it is an intuition that goes in the contrary direction: it is here in our own Middle-earth that we are frustrated because we so feebly participate in our deepest vocation.

---

12 See also Amendt-Raduege 2010.

Returning to the Elves, in light of the above we can say that they are thus excluded from true immortality, a fact that weighs them down.[13] In the post-*Rings* tale "Athrabeth Finrod ah Andreth" mentioned earlier, Finrod the High Elf is keenly aware that even death delayed for eons is no less dreaded: "it is not clear that a foreseen doom long delayed is in all ways a lighter burden than one that comes soon" (*Morgoth* 312). Moreover, life on Middle-earth eventually becomes wearying, a mere "serial longevity" (*Letters* no. 208), to use Tolkien's term. A (rare) alternative for Elves is a marriage between them and a mortal: on the one hand they "truly die", i.e. achieve "freedom from the circles of the world", on the other hand they may partake of the possibility of the human hope for eternal life in Ilúvatar. It is primarily the Elves who call death "Ilúvatar's gift to Men". The artistic construct is not without theological daring, since, as Flieger (1997:96) points out, at least on the surface the author would seem "to be subverting or contradicting his own faith by presenting death as the positive and its opposite, continued life, as the negative." However, it must be born in mind that his artistic argument rests on the principle of paradox regarding the relationship between Elves and Men.

For human beings the deathlessness of the Elves presents a powerful temptation, since it is empirical and not a matter of faith. The theme is the dominant motif of the "Akallabêth", the story of Númenor posthumously published in *The Silmarillion* and briefly recapped in the appendixes of *The Lord of the Rings*. Although Númenóreans live in a near paradise with exceedingly long life-spans at the price of willingly accepting the time of their death, with time they balk at their perceived confinement, complaining to the messenger of the Valar:

> Why should we not envy the Valar, or even the least of the Deathless? For of us is required a blind trust, and a hope without assurance, knowing not what lies before us in a little while. And yet we also love the Earth and would not lose it. (*S* Ak).

One of the signs of the Númenóreans' growing inability to accept death is their increasing practice of "build[ing] great houses for their dead" (*S* Ak). This theme is carried over into *The Lord of the Rings* where the same practice

---

13 An argument similar to the one I am going to make in the following paragraphs is presented, among others, by Kevin Aldrich 1999.

of their descendants is a sign of the decline of Minas Tirith. Thus building monuments is considered a kind of impure substitute immortality. The actual conclusion of the story of Númenor takes place in the appendixes of *The Lord of the Rings* where Aragorn accepts the time of his death voluntarily. Significantly, much like in medieval legends of saints, his body remains undecayed after death, attaining by grace what the degenerate Númenóreans attempted to carve out of stone.

If the story of Númenor together with its conclusion in *The Lord of the Rings* saga indicates the sinfulness of attempting to strive for deathlessness, this does not mean that the desire for immortality is altogether impure for Tolkien. Athrabeth, in her dialogue with Finrod, proclaims that according to the lore of her people "we knew that we had been born *never* to *die*. And by that, my lord, we meant: *born to life everlasting, without any shadow of any end*" (*Morgoth* 314). This posthumously published story is the point where Tolkien's mythology comes closest to evoking his own Christian belief, wherein traditionally death is understood as having been introduced into the world through original sin. As the ensuing dialogue indicates, deploring the intervening "darkness" that perverted its true original nature, the desire of immortality is demonstrated to stem from the intuition of the prelapsarian state of humanity, and not merely from the fear of death. And it is this paradox that needs to be stressed even if Tolkien's theology does not match some contemporary understandings.

The Middle-earth conviction that death is a "gift of Ilúvatar" and as such must be accepted ultimately stems from the belief that Ilúvatar can eventually turn the wrong doings of humanity toward a greater good. Tolkien, a believer of *felix culpa*, or the "blessed fault", expressed this sentiment in his correspondence: "A divine 'punishment' is also a divine 'gift,' if accepted, since its object is ultimate blessing, and the supreme inventiveness of the Creator will make 'punishments' [...] produce a good not otherwise to be attained" (*Letters* no. 212).

If the above can be considered Tolkien's "high" theology of death, which has rightfully attracted the lion's share of the scholars' attention, then *The Lord of the Rings* may be seen as pointing toward a noteworthy "low" theology. I have indicated in the discussion of hierarchy in Middle-earth that it helps provide structure to community. For the Christian death introduces its own hierarchy into the individual life, likewise encouraging "rightly ordering our lives" (Wood 2003a:38). As Harvard pastor Peter Gomes (2002:137) puts it, "The awareness of mortality, the first fruit of the Garden of Eden, is one of the continuing themes of self-awareness, self-discipline, and moral intelligence throughout the Bible; and the awareness of death is the first key to the discipline that contributes to the good life." This disciplining is reflected indirectly in *The Lord of the Rings*. As Anna Mathie (2003:10-11) has noted, in Tolkien's world "immortality and long life lead even the noblest creatures to a spiritual dead end, or to outright corruption." The Elves, for instance, are a fairly stagnant "antiquitarian" people, the Ents are declining, while barrenness also marks the city of Minis Tirith, home of the Númenóreans known for their longevity: Beregond, for instance, tells Pippin, "There were always too few children in the city" (*LotR* RK.V.i).

In contrast to the "high" *legendarium* where the giving up of immortality on the part of an Elf pairing with a human constitutes an exceptional fate, in *Unfinished Tales* we have the comparatively mundane Second Age story of "Aldarion and Erendis". Here the eponymous protagonists are simply separated by the long life span of an aristocratic male Númenórean while the woman he loves possesses a normal life span. She is ultimately put off by his indecision and dithering in relation to their love, rooted in the fact that he feels relatively unpressured by the passage of time, i.e. he becomes incapable of "rightly ordering his life" and consequently also ruins the life of the woman he loves.

Mathie further notes the paradox that the race least interested in longevity for its own sake offers the greatest resistance to evil, and relates it to the Hobbits' pursuit of the mortal path of immortality, i.e. parenthood:

> This fertility, this willingness to pass life onto a new generation rather than grasping for "endless life unchanging", is the Hobbits' great strength [...]. It makes them at once humbler than immortals, since they place less confidence in their own individual abilities, and more hopeful, since their own individual defeats are not the end of everything. The life that lives its life for its offspring may never achieve perfection, but neither is it ever utterly defeated. Some hope remains. (Mathie 2003:11)

We can also observe a paradox regarding the contrast between the Hobbits' zest for life and its coexistence with a simple heroism that includes a readiness to face death, as is primarily exemplified by Frodo and his companions during the War of the Ring, and our contemporary European culture. In a consumer culture that has largely lost the sense that there are any values worth dying for, heroism is often unappreciated, and it should be noted that for decades the suicide rate has steadily risen. It seems that when values worth dying for are lacking, slowly but surely the reasons for living become likewise obscured.

Although perhaps of less interest than its loftier counterpart, Tolkien's low theology of death is more down to earth and heightens the reader's awareness of the miracle of the ordinary, i.e. the sacramental dimension of existence. Moreover, one might relate both theologies through the maxim, as Flieger (1997:112) puts it: "to be capable of living is to be capable of dying, and without death there can be no rebirth." This is certainly consonant with biblical soteriology where among other things salvation means human renewal.

In this – admittedly partial – study of theological themes in Tolkien's thought and creative work and their connection with death, some general conclusions can be made. I am inclined to agree with the critic Lee Oser that with concepts like eucatastrophe and its literary embodiment in *The Lord of the Rings* Tolkien achieves "a fine theological rapprochement between his Augustinian sense of our fallenness and his Thomistic confidence in our 'bents and faculties'" (Oser 2008:59). One might say he finds a *modus vivendi* between the dialectical and analogical sides of his religious imagination.

In Tolkien's Middle-earth mythology and *legendarium* there is a graduated shift in focus from the cosmological to the human and mundane; nevertheless, the "deep (or religious) narrative" continues to undergird the "surface narrative"[14] of *The Lord of the Rings*, which contributes to its surprising depth. Even if the religious nature of Tolkien's "deep narrative" escapes many readers, not a few of them feel changed. This is largely an effect of the hope conveyed by Tolkien's profound Christian humanism embedded in the comedic narrative. "The distinction of Christian humanism is its focus, which is the human person in light of his or her vocation within the cre-

---

14 A distinction made by Fleming Rutledge, see Rutledge (2004:3). In his "theological narrative" analysis of *The Lord of the Rings* Rutledge reads the novel as a theological thriller.

ated order" (Bequette 2007:xiv) – and this certainly marks Middle-earth fiction.

Returning to the puzzle of Tolkien's comedic theology of narrative and its clash with the major theme of death in *The Lord of the Rings*, perhaps some insight can be gained by suggesting that, in a manner similar to Aquinas's anagogical level of scriptural interpretation, the real "joyous turn" in Tolkien's opus should be sought at an eschatological level. Alison Milbank (2009:112) summarizes this view: "Tolkien [...] leaves us within the paradoxical, with the epiphany to work out for ourselves." A transcendent eucatastrophe is proposed but not imposed on the reader.

In a theological reading of Tolkien, vocation implies a *telos* to human affairs. The horizontal transcendence of vocation ultimately points to the vertical transcendence where human flourishing is radically enhanced. Moreover, "Through the power of his mythic imagination", as Stratford Caldecott (1999:26) puts it, "Tolkien evoked the tragedy and mystery of death against the backdrop of an even greater mystery: that of existence itself." Which is why a theology of death and a theology of life are so closely interrelated.

About the Author

CHRISTOPHER GARBOWSKI is an associate professor at the Department of English at Maria Curie-Skłodowska University, Poland. He is the author of a number of books, including *Recovery and Transcendence for the Contemporary Mythmaker: The Spiritual Dimension in the Works of JRR Tolkien* (2000) and *Spiritual Values in Peter Jackson's The Lord of the Rings* (2005).

Bibliography

ALDRICH, Kevin. 1999. "The Sense of Time in Tolkien's *The Lord of the Rings*." In Joseph PEARCE (ed.). 1999. *Tolkien: A Celebration*. London: HarperCollins, 86-101.

AMENDT-RADUEGE, Amy. 2010. "Better off Dead: The Lesson of the Ringwraiths." In Thomas HONEGGER & Fanfan CHEN (eds.). 2010. *Immortals and the Undead*. (*Fastitocalon* 1.1). Trier: WVT, 69-82.

ARMSTRONG, Helen. 1998. "There Are Two People in This Marriage." *Mallorn* 36:10-12.

BACHMANN, Dieter. 2007. "Words for Magic: *goetia*, *gûl*, and *lúth*." In Eduardo SEGURA and Thomas HONEGGER (eds.). 2007. *Myth and Magic. Art according to the Inklings*. Zurich and Berne: Walking Tree Publishers, 47-55.

BASSHAM, Gregory & Eric BRONSON (eds.). 2003. *The Lord of the Rings and Philosophy*. Chicago and La Salle, IL: Open Court.

BEQUETTE, John. 2007. *Christian Humanism: Creation, Redemption, and Reintegration*. Lanham, MD: University Press of America.

CALDECOTT, Stratford. 1999. "Over the Chasm of Fire: Christian Heroism in *The Silmarillion* and *The Lord of the Rings*." In Joseph PEARCE (ed.). 1999. *Tolkien: A Celebration*. London: HarperCollins, 17-33.

CARPENTER, Humphrey. 2002. *J.R.R. Tolkien: A Biography*. London: HarperCollins.

CURRY, Patrick. 1999. "Magic vs. Enchantment." *Journal of Contemporary Religion* 14:401-412.

DAVIS, Bill. 2003. "Choosing to Die: The Gift of Mortality in Middle-earth." In Gregory BASSHAM & Eric BRONSON (eds.). 2003. *The Lord of the Rings and Philosophy*. Chicago and La Salle, IL: Open Court, 123-136.

ELBERSTADT, Mary. 2007. "How the West Really Lost God." *Policy Review* 143:12-13.

ELKIN, James & David MORGAN (eds.). 2008. *Re-Enchantment*. New York: Routledge.

FLIEGER, Verlyn. 1997. *A Question of Time: J.R.R. Tolkien's Road to Faerie*. Kent, OH: Kent State University Press.

2002. *Splintered Light. Logos and Language in Tolkien's World*. Kent, OH: Kent State University Press.

GARBOWSKI, Christopher. 2003. "Tolkien's Middle Earth and the Catholic Imagination." *Mallorn* 61:9-12.

GOMES, Peter J. 2002. *The Good Life: Truths That Last in Times of Need*. New York: Harper Collins.

GREELEY, Andrew. 2000. *The Catholic Imagination*. Berkeley: University of California Press.

HEAD, Hayden. 2007. "Imitative Desire in Tolkien's Mythology: A Girardian Perspective." *Mythlore* 26.1-2:137-148.

HIBBS, Thomas. 2003. "Providence and the Dramatic Unity of *The Lord of the Rings*." In Gregory BASSHAM & Eric BRONSON (eds.). 2003. *The Lord of the Rings and Philosophy*. Chicago and La Salle, IL: Open Court, 167-178.

HUTTON, Ronald. "The Pagan Tolkien." In Sarah WELLS (ed.). 2008. *The Ring Goes Ever On. Proceedings of the Tolkien 2005 Conference '50 Years of The Lord of the Rings'*. Coventry, UK: The Tolkien Society, vol. 2, 32-39.

HUIZINGA, Johan. 2002. *Homo Ludens: A Study of the Play Element in Culture*. London: Routledge and Kegan Paul.

MATHIE, Anna. 2003. "Tolkien and the Gift of Mortality." *First Things* 137:10-11.

MCMAHON, Darrin M. 2006. *Happiness: A History*. New York: Atlantic Monthly Press.

MILBANK, Alison. 2009. *Chesterton and Tolkien as Theologians: The Fantasy of the Real*. London: T&T Clark.

MORGAN, David. 2008. "Art and Religion in the Modern Age." In James ELKIN & David MORGAN (eds.). 2008. *Re-Enchantment*. New York: Routledge, 25-46.

OSER, Lee. 2008. *The Return of Christian Humanism: Chesterton, Eliot, Tolkien and the Romance of History*. Columbia, MO: University of Missouri Press.

PEARCE, Joseph (ed.). 1999. *Tolkien: A Celebration*. London: HarperCollins.

ROSEBURY, Brian. 2003. *Tolkien: A Cultural Phenomenon*. Basingstoke: Palgrave Macmillan.

RUTLEDGE, Fleming. 2004. *The Battle for Middle-earth: Tolkien's Divine Design in The Lord of the Rings*. Grand Rapids, MI: Eerdmans.

SHIPPEY, Tom. 2005. *The Road to Middle-earth*. London: HarperCollins.

TAYLOR, Charles. 2007. *A Secular Age*. Cambridge, MA: The Belknap Press of Harvard University Press.

WELLS, Sarah (ed.). 2008. *The Ring Goes Ever On. Proceedings of the Tolkien 2005 Conference '50 Years of The Lord of the Rings'*. Coventry, UK: The Tolkien Society.

WOOD, Ralph. 2003a. *The Gospel According to Tolkien: Visions of the Kingdom in Middle-earth*. Louisville, KY: Westminster John Knox Press.

2003b. "Conflict and Convergence on Fundamental Matters in C.S. Lewis and J.R.R. Tolkien." *Renascence* 55.4:315-328.

ZIMBARDO, Rose A. 2004. "Moral Vision in *The Lord of the Rings*." In Rose A. ZIMBARDO & Neil D. ISAACS (eds.). 2004. *Understanding The Lord of the Rings: The Best of Tolkien Criticism*. Boston and New York: Houghton Mifflin, 68-75.

& Neil D. ISAACS (eds.). 2004. *Understanding The Lord of the Rings: The Best of Tolkien Criticism*. Boston and New York: Houghton Mifflin.

Works by J.R.R. Tolkien

Letters: *The Letters of J.R.R. Tolkien*, ed. Humphrey Carpenter, with the assistance of Christopher Tolkien. London: George Allen & Unwin, 1981.

LotR: *The Lord of the Rings*, 50th anniversary edition, Boston: Houghton Mifflin, 2004.

MC: *The Monsters and the Critics and Other Essays*, ed. Christopher Tolkien. London: George Allen & Unwin 1983. London: HarperCollins, 1997.

Morgoth: *Morgoth's Ring* (HoMe 10), ed. Christopher Tolkien. London: George Allen & Unwin 1993.

S: *The Silmarillion*, ed. Christopher Tolkien, London: George Allen & Unwin, 1977; reprinted London: HarperCollins, 2001.

Giampaolo Canzonieri

Tolkien at King Edward's School

The Documents

The Committee behind this book considered it appropriate to present some documents connected with Tolkien's own early studies in the field. We therefore contacted King Edward's School, the Birmingham institution attended by Tolkien in his youth, and asked whether they could provide a document related to the subject. The Headmaster of King Edward's School, Mr John Claughton, promptly responded to our request and kindly agreed to make available two documents that, despite their brevity, provide an interesting glimpse into Tolkien's school life.

The first document describes the organisation of the curriculum as it was established in 1906. Although its language is that of an impersonal official document, it nonetheless provides a glimpse of the world which the young JRR Tolkien entered rather abruptly in September 1900. He must still have pined for the rural village of Sarehole where he had spent the most beautiful and serene period of his life.

The second document is more directly related to the future philologist, professor and author. At that time, Tolkien was merely a pupil at King Edward's but with hopes of entering the University of Oxford if his academic performance was good enough. The document is an official report by the Oxford and Cambridge Schools Examination Board, a joint committee established by the two historical universities to examine pupils attending the final classes of Secondary School. The task of the Examination Board was to evaluate the pupils' level of academic achievement and to spot promising young men whom they would encourage and, when needed, also support financially by means of scholarships.[1] The

---

1 The Oxford and Cambridge Schools Examination Board was established in 1873, taking over what were previously the separate responsibilities of the Delegacy for the Inspection and Examination of Schools of Oxford University and the Schools Examination Syndicate of Cambridge University. The Board operated continuously for more than a century, and was dissolved only in 1995.

performance report of Class 1 in the work on Roman history assigned by the Examination Board in August 1911 explicitly mentions Tolkien – as well as his friend Rob Gilson, a prominent figure in his emotional universe.[2] The report, in spite of the mentioning Tolkien only briefly, not only renders him recognizable but confirms those characteristics that will become the hallmarks of the adult and mature Tolkien as he emerges from his published works and letters. Knowing in particular Tolkien's tendency to jump abruptly from one work to another – leaving many of them incomplete in order to revise or rewrite them sometimes many years later – it is particularly striking that the examiners' note claims that candidate Tolkien "was also very irrelevant".

Tolkien at King Edward's School

Mabel Tolkien enters young John Ronald at King Edward's School a first time in September 1900, sending him to the same institution his father, whom he had lost early in childhood, had attended many years before. The course of study at King Edward's at the time consisted of a series of classes whose sequence was not strictly fixed, the pupils having the option of skipping some of them altogether. Classes were numbered in decreasing order starting from the thirteenth, the initial one, and ending with the first, after which the pupils graduated and left the school. The eighth class, however, was followed by three unnumbered ones known as "Lower Remove", "Upper Remove" and "Transitus", after which the pupils could choose a Classic/Literary or a Modern/Scientific side.[3] Entered into the eleventh class when eight and a half years old, young Tolkien finds himself in the eighth only just one year after, but having to move with his family from King's Heath to Edgbaston he leaves the school at the age of ten at the beginning of the year 1902. One year and a few months later, in the spring of 1903, he comes back to stay and, thanks to a scholarship, is entered in the Lower Remove that he leaves in the autumn of the same year to pass,

---

2 Robert Quilter Gilson ("Rob"), son of the Headmaster of King Edward's School, was, together with Geoffrey Bache Smith and Christopher Wiseman, Tolkien's best friend during his youth. The four of them were the founders of the Tea Club Barrovian Society (TCBS). Gilson and Smith both died at the Battle of the Somme in the Great War, leaving the two surviving friends with a sense of bereavement that took years to overcome (see John Garth's masterly study of Tolkien's formative years).
3 In today's King Edward's the two Removes are still present, corresponding to the eighth year of the English standard National Curriculum.

barely twelve years old, directly to the sixth class of the Classic/Literary side – classes numbering proceeding in a very peculiar way with the seventh for the Modern/Scientific side and the sixth for the Classic/Literary side.

In young Tolkien's times King Edward's School could not yet count two Nobel Prize and one Fields Medal winners among their *alumni*[4] – not to mention a world famous philologist and writer – but it had already been the school attended by several important personalities and had acquired a reputation that made it the natural choice for a well-born, if not exactly wealthy, boy who showed signs of a promising inclination for languages. King Edward's was then located in New Street, quite in the city centre. It had been founded in 1552, and during the reign of Edward VII it was Birmingham's primary grammar school in a period that was soon perceived to be a kind of golden age for arts and culture. During this "Edwardian" period the level of education of the middle and upper classes was so high that a boy attending the first class and ready to graduate from a school such as King Edward's would be able to speak fluently French, had equally mastered Latin and Greek and would be deeply versed in other languages he may have studied for his own pleasure, such did Tolkien with Anglo-Saxon and Gothic. The polyglot competence becomes visible in the fact that Tolkien's and 1911 first classes' farewell to King Edward's was celebrated by performing Aristophanes' "The Peace" in Ancient Greek, followed by "God Save the King" sung in chorus in that same language. To think that about half of this gifted generation, so full of culture, values and ideals, was soon going to meet their death in the Great War, still imbues a sense of discomfort. It makes us wonder how many masterpieces of art, be they novels, poems, or paintings, were buried forever with their would-have-been authors in the mud of the Somme.

---

4 Respectively, Maurice H.F. Wilkins, Nobel Prize in Physiology or Medicine 1962, John R. Vane, same in 1982, and Richard E. Borcherds, Fields Medal in 1998. We are also pleased to mention that Mr Tom Shippey, whose contribution to the "Tolkien and Philosophy" meeting is included in this book, studied at King Edward's School which he left with the 1960 first classes.

Document 1

King Edward's School, Birmingham: curriculum early 20th century

The nine classes from the Thirteenth upwards to the Transitus, inclusive, receive instruction in the ordinary elementary subjects of a liberal education, viz., Arithmetic and Elementary Mathematics, Scripture, English History, Geography, French, Latin and Drawing. The boys are also (as far as Class VIII) instructed in Botany, with the intention of training their powers of observation and evoking an interest in the objects and phenomena of Nature. In the Removes and Transitus Botany is replaced by the beginning of a systematic course in Physics and Chemistry. All boys throughout the school are required to take physical exercises in the Gymnasium, unless forbidden to do so by a medical man.

Above the Transitus, the average of which is about 14, though an able boy will usually pass through it quite a year earlier than that, the School is divided into a Classical or Literary, and Modern, or, rather, Scientific Side. The Modern Side do not learn Greek nor (except in a Voluntary Class) do the Classical Side learn Sciences. The amount of time given to Mathematics on both Sides is the same and Modern Languages are also studied on both Sides. Boys who have any prospect of proceeding to Oxford or Cambridge should take the Classical Side, and it is especially desirable that the boys who show Mathematical promise should do so. All who contemplate a Degree in arts at any university will naturally take this Side, and a good many others who do not fall under the above heads will be found to do well there. It is easier to transfer a boy from the Classical to the Modern Sides than vice versa. On the other hand, boys who show distinct scientific or engineering proclivities should be on the Modern Side, and so will all who contemplate a course (in any faculty but that of Arts) at one of the newer Universities. The Science Department of the School is equipped in the most complete and modern manner, the buildings including a Chemical Laboratory, two Physical Laboratories, a Biological Laboratory, two Lecture Rooms, and other appurtenances.

Document 2

**Oxford and Cambridge Schools Examination Board
Report on King Edward's School, Birmingham
August 1911**

Ancient History

The work of Class 1 on Roman history reached a good average, without any remarkable brilliance. Most of the candidates seemed to understand how to answer a history question. They made good points, but were often satisfied merely to enlarge on the one without making the answer complete. The best work was undoubtedly done by Gilson in both papers; he shewed that he possessed a considerable knowledge of the history and he used his knowledge in the right manner. Faulconbridge and Barrowclough were also very fair, and shewed considerable promise. Tolkien gave signs of a more acute and independent judgement than anyone else; his style also was more matured, but he seemed to have no control over it and sometimes became almost unintelligible; he was also very irrelevant, particularly on the Special Period, in which he only attempted four questions. In this paper, he with many others made the mistake of giving the details of all Caesar's campaigns in Gaul, when the question only asked for one campaign.

About the Author

Giampaolo CANZONIERI obtained a degree in Computer Science and earns his living in this field. He discovered *The Lord of the Rings* at the age of fifteen and Tolkien has been part of his life ever since. He is a member of the committee that stands behind the Italian *Tolkien e dintorni* book series, to which he contributed first by participating in the translation of Tom Shippey's *The Road to Middle-earth* and then by supervising the translation of Joseph Pearce's *Tolkien: Man and Myth* and of *La Trasmissione del pensiero e la numerazione degli elfi*, a collection including J.R.R. Tolkien's "Ósanwe-kenta", "Notes on Óre" and "Eldarin Hands, Fingers and Numerals".

Bibliography

GARTH, John. 2003. *Tolkien and the Great War*, London: HarperCollins.

Index

A
Aragorn
    his death 138
Ariosto, Lodovico 52
Arthur of Britain 32
Aristotle 34, 50
St Augustine (of Hippo) 27, 50, 58

B
Barfield, Owen 74f, 82
    Poetic Diction 74
de Beauvoir, Simone
    on death 125
Bilbo
    epithets 78
beauty and truth 110
Beowulf 46
Bloomsbury Group 52f
Boethius, Boethian 27, 32, 50, 55, 57f, 61, 65, 95
    De Consolatione Philosophiae 55, 65
    Old English Boethius 32f
Boiardo, Matteo 52

C
Caritt, E.F. 28f
    Theory of Beauty (1914) 28
Cassirer, Ernst 74f, 82
    Sprache und Mythos 74
Chance, chance 59-61, 63
Chesterton, Gilbert K. 88f
Collingwood, Robin 29, 31
Collingwood, W.G. 31
courage 115, 120
    Byrhtnoth 116
    Hobbits 117f
    Túrin 115
Croce, Benedetto 34, 50

D
death
    as the 'gift of Ilúvatar' 137f
    for human beings and Elves 126, 136, 137
deathlessness
    of Elves 136f
    of Ringwraiths 136
Derrida, Jacques 81

E
Eliot, George
    Silas Marner (1861) 65
Elves
    the different categories and types of Elves 75f
Elvish
    Quenya 75, 80
    Sindarin 75, 77, 80
enchantment/disenchantment/re-enchantment 130
Entish 79f
eucatastrophe 113, 129, 135
existentialism
    German and French existentialism 22

F
fate 59f
felix culpa
    'the blessed fault' 138
Flieger, Verlyn
    A Question of Time: J.R.R. Tolkien's Road to Faërie (1997) 136f, 140
    Splintered Light. Logos and Language in Tolkien's World (2002) 129
folly/foolishness 103
Forster, E.M. 52f
free will 60
friendship
    between Sam and Frodo 134

G
Gilson, Rob 146
Gomes, Peter J.
    The Good Life: Truths That Last in Times of Need (2002) 139
Good vs. Evil 57f, 95
the Gospels 129

Greely, Andrew
    The Catholic Imagination (2000) 128, 132f
Greene, Graham 90
Grimm, Jacob 24, 36f

H
heroes 115-117, 119
historicism 35
Hobbits
    and community 133
    and death 139
    as misfits in Middle-earth 112, 114
    as representatives of a Christian ethos and humility 98-102, 104
Holy Trinity 85f
Howard, Robert E. 102
Huizinga, Johan
    Homo Ludens: A Study of the Play Element in Culture (1939) 131
humility 113
humour 118

I
idealism
    German idealism 22
Ilúvatar 132f
imagination
    analogical and dialectical imaginations 128, 134
    Catholic imagination 128, 133
    theistic imagination 128
Inklings 26, 29, 53, 74

J
James, William 25
Joachim, Harold 29
joy 111, 113

K
Kalevala 78
King Edward's School 145-149

L
language 74f, 78f
Lewis, C.S. 43, 49, 128, 133
    That Hideous Strength (1945) 41

Lórien 79-83
    Entish name 79
ludology 131
luck 62-64

M
MacDonald, George 92
Manichaeus, Manichean 57f, 95, 134
Men
    and death 137
    Númenóreans 137
Middle-earth 133, 135f
    hierarchical structure 132
Milbank, Alison
    Chesterton and Tolkien as Theologians: The Fantasy of the Real (2009) 129, 132, 134, 141
Minas Tirith 138
Moore, G.E.
    Principia Ethica (1903) 52
Myers, J.N.L. 32
mythology
    comparative mythology 35
    and language 73f, 82
mythopoesis 88, 96

N
Northern theory of courage, Northern courage 98, 116

O
O'Connor, Flannery 88f, 92
Oser, Lee
    The Return of Christian Humanism: Chesterton, Eliot, Tolkien and the Romance of History (2008) 140

P
paganism 103f
palantiri
    and their 'fateful' role in the War of the Ring 64
parables (of Christ) 89
Pasternak, Boris
    Doctor Zhivago 89
philologists
    as scrutinisers 25

philology
    as contrast to philosophy 22
    Classical philology 24
    comparative philology 23-25
philosophers
    not mentioned by Tolkien 21
    not influencing Tolkien 44f
    as generalisers 25
    influencing philologists 35-41
    Romanticist philosophers influencing Tolkien 51
philosophia perennis 21
philosophy
    and the great questions of human life 26
    Lady Philosophy (in Boethius) 55-58, 61
    Oxbridge analytical philosophy 22
    word used in Tolkien's work of fiction 21f
    word used in Tolkien's other writings 21f
Plato 27, 30, 50
    Gorgias 27
    on power 120-122
    Phaedo 27
    Republic 27
    Timaeus 27
Providence 55-65, 91, 104

Q
Quendi
    see Elves

R
The Red Book of Westmarch 108
Romanticism
    German Romanticism 74
Russell, Bertrand
    Principia Mathematica (3 volumes, 1910-13) 52
Rutledge, Fleming
    The Battle for Middle-earth: Tolkien's Divine Design in The Lord of the Rings (2004) 125

S
Sapir, Edward 74f, 82
    Sapir-Whorf hypothesis 74
Schopenhauer, Arthur 29, 50

Second Music of the Ainur 136
Shakespeare, William
   Macbeth 31
   A Midsummer Night's Dream 31
Smith, J.A. 29
Snorri Sturluson
   Prose Edda 30
stories
   their effect 105-108
sub-creation 88, 96, 129-131
'survivor genres' (fairy-tales, nursery-rhymes, riddles) 54

T

Thomas Aquinas 27, 50, 88
   on happiness 129
   Summa Theologiae 28
Thomas Malory
   Le Morte D'Arthur (1474) 52
Tolkien, John Ronald Reuel
   'Aldarion and Erendis' 139
   as a Catholic 85
   as a Christian philologist 47
   as a critic of his own work 87, 92
   as a Germanic philologist 47
   as an orphan 45, 53
   as a nationalist 46
   as a philosopher 85
   as (Christian/Catholic) storyteller/narrator/writer 86, 88f, 95
   'Athrabeth Finrod ah Andreth' 27f, 126, 137
   '*Beowulf*: The Monsters and the Critics' 82, 129
   education at King Edward's School 145-149
   The Hobbit 75, 78, 81f
   'Leaf by Niggle' 126
   The Legend of Sigurd and Gudrún 31, 51
   The Lord of the Rings 75-77, 79f, 82
      and evil 134f
      death as a major theme 125, 127, 135
      the theme of community 133
   'On Fairy-Stories' 73, 129
   The Silmarillion 75
Tom Bombadil 76-78, 82f
Tracy, David, 128

Treebeard the Ent
    naming things 78

V
Valar 133, 137
Vico, Giambattista 35
virtue
    private virtue 53
    public virtue 53
Vonnegut, Kurt
    Cat's Cradle (1963) 26

W
Wagner, Richard
    Der Ring des Nibelungen 31, 51
Weber, Max 130
Whorf, Benjamin Lee
    see Sapir
Wilson, Cook 29
wyrd 63

Walking Tree Publishers

Walking Tree Publishers was founded in 1997 as a forum for publication of material (books, videos, CDs, etc.) related to Tolkien and Middle-earth studies.

Please also visit our web pages:
http://www.walking-tree.org

Walking Tree Publishers are based in Zurich and Jena.

Cormarë Series

The *Cormarë Series* collects papers and studies dedicated exclusively to the exploration of Tolkien's work. It comprises monographs, thematic collections of essays, conference volumes, and reprints of important yet no longer (easily) accessible papers by leading scholars in the field. Manuscripts and project proposals are evaluated by members of an independent board of advisors who support the series editors in their endeavour to provide the readers with qualitatively superior yet accessible studies on Tolkien and his work.

News from the Shire and Beyond. Studies on Tolkien
Peter Buchs and Thomas Honegger (eds.), Zurich and Berne 2004, Reprint, First edition 1997 (Cormarë Series 1), ISBN 978-3-9521424-5-5

Root and Branch. Approaches Towards Understanding Tolkien
Thomas Honegger (ed.), Zurich and Berne 2005, Reprint, First edition 1999 (Cormarë Series 2), ISBN 978-3-905703-01-6

Richard Sturch, *Four Christian Fantasists. A Study of the Fantastic Writings of George MacDonald, Charles Williams, C.S. Lewis and J.R.R. Tolkien*
Zurich and Berne 2007, Reprint, First edition 2001 (Cormarë Series 3), ISBN 978-3-905703-04-7

Tolkien in Translation
Thomas Honegger (ed.), Zurich and Jena 2011, Reprint, First edition 2003 (Cormarë Series 4), ISBN 978-3-905703-15-3

Mark T. Hooker, *Tolkien Through Russian Eyes*
Zurich and Berne 2003 (Cormarë Series 5), ISBN 978-3-9521424-7-9

Translating Tolkien: Text and Film
Thomas Honegger (ed.), Zurich and Jena 2011, Reprint, First edition 2004 (Cormarë Series 6), ISBN 978-3-905703-16-0

Christopher Garbowski, *Recovery and Transcendence for the Contemporary Mythmaker. The Spiritual Dimension in the Works of J.R.R. Tolkien*
Zurich and Berne 2004, Reprint, First Edition by Marie Curie Sklodowska, University Press, Lublin 2000, (Cormarë Series 7), ISBN 978-3-9521424-8-6

Reconsidering Tolkien
Thomas Honegger (ed.), Zurich and Berne 2005 (Cormarë Series 8), ISBN 978-3-905703-00-9

Tolkien and Modernity 1
Frank Weinreich and Thomas Honegger (eds.), Zurich and Berne 2006 (Cormarë Series 9), ISBN 978-3-905703-02-3

Tolkien and Modernity 2
Thomas Honegger and Frank Weinreich (eds.), Zurich and Berne 2006 (Cormarë Series 10), ISBN 978-3-905703-03-0

Tom Shippey, *Roots and Branches. Selected Papers on Tolkien by Tom Shippey*
Zurich and Berne 2007 (Cormarë Series 11), ISBN 978-3-905703-05-4

Ross Smith, *Inside Language. Linguistic and Aesthetic Theory in Tolkien*
Zurich and Jena 2011, Reprint, First edition 2007 (Cormarë Series 12), ISBN 978-3-905703-20-7

How We Became Middle-earth. A Collection of Essays on The Lord of the Rings
Adam Lam and Nataliya Oryshchuk (eds.), Zurich and Berne 2007 (Cormarë Series 13), ISBN 978-3-905703-07-8

Myth and Magic. Art According to the Inklings
Eduardo Segura and Thomas Honegger (eds.), Zurich and Berne 2007 (Cormarë Series 14), ISBN 978-3-905703-08-5

The Silmarillion - Thirty Years On
Allan Turner (ed.), Zurich and Berne 2007 (Cormarë Series 15), ISBN 978-3-905703-10-8

Martin Simonson, *The Lord of the Rings and the Western Narrative Tradition*
Zurich and Jena 2008 (Cormarë Series 16), ISBN 978-3-905703-09-2

Tolkien's Shorter Works. Proceedings of the 4th Seminar of the Deutsche Tolkien Gesellschaft & Walking Tree Publishers Decennial Conference
Margaret Hiley and Frank Weinreich (eds.), Zurich and Jena 2008 (Cormarë Series 17), ISBN 978-3-905703-11-5

Tolkien's The Lord of the Rings: Sources of Inspiration
Stratford Caldecott and Thomas Honegger (eds.), Zurich and Jena 2008 (Cormarë Series 18), ISBN 978-3-905703-12-2

J.S. Ryan, *Tolkien's View: Windows into his World*
Zurich and Jena 2009 (Cormarë Series 19), ISBN 978-3-905703-13-9

Music in Middle-earth
Heidi Steimel and Friedhelm Schneidewind (eds.), Zurich and Jena 2010 (Cormarë Series 20), ISBN 978-3-905703-14-6

Liam Campbell, *The Ecological Augury in the Works of JRR Tolkien*
Zurich and Jena 2011 (Cormarë Series 21), ISBN 978-3-905703-18-4

Margaret Hiley, *The Loss and the Silence. Aspects of Modernism in the Works of C.S. Lewis, J.R.R. Tolkien and Charles Williams*
Zurich and Jena 2011 (Cormarë Series 22), ISBN 978-3-905703-19-1

Rainer Nagel, *Hobbit Place-names. A Linguistic Excursion through the Shire*
Zurich and Jena 2012 (Cormarë Series 23), ISBN 978-3-905703-22-1

Christopher MacLachlan, *Tolkien and Wagner: The Ring and Der Ring*
Zurich and Jena 2012 (Cormarë Series 24), ISBN 978-3-905703-21-4

Renée Vink, *Wagner and Tolkien: Mythmakers*
Zurich and Jena 2012 (Cormarë Series 25), ISBN 978-3-905703-25-2

The Broken Scythe. Death and Immortality in the Works of J.R.R. Tolkien
Roberto Arduini and Claudio Antonio Testi (eds.), Zurich and Jena 2012
(Cormarë Series 26), ISBN 978-3-905703-26-9

Sub-creating Middle-earth: Constructions of Authorship and the Works of J.R.R. Tolkien
Judith Klinger (ed.), Zurich and Jena 2012 (Cormarë Series 27),
ISBN 978-3-905703-27-6

Tolkien's Poetry
Julian Eilmann and Allan Turner (eds.), Zurich and Jena 2013
(Cormarë Series 28), ISBN 978-3-905703-28-3

O, What a Tangled Web. Tolkien and Medieval Literature. A View from Poland
Barbara Kowalik (ed.), Zurich and Jena 2013 (Cormarë Series 29),
ISBN 978-3-905703-29-0

J.S. Ryan, *In the Nameless Wood*
Zurich and Jena 2013 (Cormarë Series 30), ISBN 978-3-905703-30-6

From Peterborough to Faëry; The Poetics and Mechanics of Secondary Worlds
Thomas Honegger & Dirk Vanderbeke (eds.), Zurich and Jena 2014
(Cormarë Series 31), ISBN 978-3-905703-31-3

Tolkien and Philosophy
Roberto Arduini and Claudio R. Testi (eds.), Zurich and Jena 2014
(Cormarë Series 32), ISBN 978-3-905703-32-0

Paul H. Kocher, *The Three Ages of Middle-earth*
Zurich and Jena, forthcoming

Beowulf and the Dragon

The original Old English text of the 'Dragon Episode' of *Beowulf* is set in an authentic font and printed and bound in hardback creating a high quality art book. Illustrated by Anke Eissmann and accompanied by John Porter's translation. Introduction by Tom Shippey. Limited first edition of 500 copies. 84 pages.

This high-quality book will please both Tolkien fans and those interested in mythology and Old English. It is also well suited as a gift.

Selected pages can be previewed on: www.walking-tree.org/beowulf

Beowulf and the Dragon
Zurich and Jena 2009
ISBN 978-3-905703-17-7

Tales of Yore Series

The *Tales of Yore Series* provides a platform for qualitatively superior fiction that will appeal to readers familiar with Tolkien's world.

Kay Woollard, *The Terror of Tatty Walk. A Frightener*
CD and Booklet, Zurich and Berne 2000, ISBN 978-3-9521424-2-4

Kay Woollard, *Wilmot's Very Strange Stone or What came of building "snobbits"*
CD and booklet, Zurich and Berne 2001, ISBN 978-3-9521424-4-8

Edward S. Louis, *The Monster Specialist*, Zurich and Jena 2014, forthcoming

Information for authors

Authors interested in contributing to our publications can learn more about the services we offer by reading the "services for authors" section of our web pages.

http://www.walking-tree.org/authors

Manuscripts and project proposals can be submitted to the board of editors (please include an SAE):

Walking Tree Publishers
CH-3052 Zollikofen
Switzerland
e-mail: info@walking-tree.org

Walking Tree Publishers, Zurich and Jena, 2014

www.ingramcontent.com/pod-product-compliance
Lightning Source LLC
Chambersburg PA
CBHW070919180426
43192CB00038B/1859